T

The Road

**based on the novel by
Cormac McCarthy**

Joe Penhall

Activities by
Paul Bunyan and Ruth Moore

Critical Scripts & Series Editors
Paul Bunyan and Ruth Moore

Methuen Drama

Published by Methuen Drama 2011

1 3 5 7 9 10 8 6 4 2

Methuen Drama
A & C Black Publishers Limited
36 Soho Square
London W1D 3QY
www.methuendrama.com

Screenplay by Joe Penhall. Copyright © 2010 by 2929 Productions LLC. First published
by Methuen Drama in 2010.
Adapted by Joe Penhall from the novel by Cormac McCarthy, published in 2006 by
Knopf. All rights reserved.

Teaching activities copyright © Methuen Drama 2011

Joe Penhall, Paul Bunyan and Ruth Moore hereby assert their rights under the Copyright,
Designs and Patents Act 1988 to be identified as the authors of this work
Images from the film *The Road*, 2009 (dir. John Hillcoat) reproduced courtesy
of Dimension Films

ISBN 978 1 408 13482 5

A CIP catalogue record for this book is available from the British Library

Typeset by MPS Limited, a Macmillan Company
Printed and bound in Great Britain by CPI Cox & Wyman Ltd, Reading, Berkshire

The Road

The Road was released in the USA on 25 November 2009 and in the UK on 8 January 2010, presented by Dimension Films and 2929 Productions. The cast was as follows:

Man	Viggo Mortensen
Boy	Kodi Smit-McPhee
Old Man	Robert Duvall
Veteran	Guy Pearce
Motherly Woman	Molly Parker
Thief	Michael Kenneth Williams
Gang Member	Garret Dillahunt
Woman	Charlize Theron
Bearded Man	Bob Jennings
Bearded Face	Kirk Brown
Bearded Man 2	Jack Erdie
Man on Mattress	David August Lindauer
Well Fed Woman	Gina Preciado
Well Fed Woman 2	Mary Rawson

Director John Hillcoat
Screenplay Joe Penhall
Producers Nick Wechsler, Paula Mae Schwartz and Steve Schwartz
Director of Photography Javier Aguirresarobe, AEC
Music Nick Cave and Warren Ellis
Editor Jon Gregory, ACE
Production Designer Chris Kennedy
Costume Designer Margot Wilson
Casting Director Francine Maisler
Stunt Coordinators Mark Donaldson and Mike Watson

EXT. CORN FIELD – DAY

The intense buzzing of summer insects and the song of songbirds.
A bird's eye view of a bucolic midwest farming landscape: corn
field, blue skies, sunshine, a **Farmer** *ploughing a nearby field*
with a tractor, grain silos and a haystack.

A **Man** *with a horse. A clapboard house with a strawberry field;*
a **Woman**'s *hand picks strawberries. A* **Woman** *lying in the*
grass, lazing.

Opening Credits

INT. DINING ROOM/HOME – NIGHT

Next to bookshelves, an upright piano, with sheet music on the
stand – Chopin. There is also a dining-room table with leftovers
from an abandoned meal – strawberries and cream.

INT. BEDROOM – NIGHT

A month later – a warm night; the **Man** *is asleep with the same*
Woman, *now pregnant, no sheets on the bed. The* **Man** *is*
restless and wakes. A distant rumbling, indistinct – the **Man**
swings his feet off the bed and goes to the window, anxious.

INT. BATHROOM – NIGHT

The **Man** *is in his shorts, sweating, putting a plug in the*
bath and turning on the taps as far as they will go. The
Woman *appears in the doorway in a nightdress and leans*
against the door frame watching, blearily, cradling her
pregnant belly.

Woman   Why are you taking a bath?

Man   I'm not.

The **Woman** *takes off her nightdress and goes to the bath.*

Woman   You'll sleep better.

He looks at her, surprised she's misunderstood.

Man   I'm not. Put your clothes back on.

She sees he's looking out the window now – there's an eerie rose-coloured glow of distant fire through the glass, and distant shouts and screams.

Woman   What is it? What is happening?

End of flashback.

Title: The Road

EXT. CAMPSITE – PRE-DAWN

A **Man** *of about forty and a* **Boy** *of ten are asleep, camped on a tarp under a rock ledge, the blackened chasm of a burnt valley spread out below. It is the same man as earlier, but ten years older, thinner, malnourished, with a thick beard.They are both emaciated and exhausted, their faces and hands coated in grime and soot from the burned, blackened landscape around them. Their hair is greasy and straggly and the man has a scraggly beard. Ash falls on the tarp, which is bright blue, the only colour in sight.*

The **Man** *is woken by something; he instinctively reaches out to touch the* **Boy***, his hand rests on his chest and rises and falls with each of the sleeping* **Boy***'s breaths.*

There is a low rumble, the ground starts to tremble and the **Boy** *wakes.*

Boy   Papa?

No reply.

Papa?

Man   Shh. It's okay.

Boy   What is it, Papa?
They listen as it grows nearer and louder, everything shaking, tree roots groaning and splitting, until it passes between them with a roar like a subway train right beneath them. The **Boy** *is*

*now clinging to the **Man** and crying, his head buried against
the **Man**'s chest in fear.*

Man   Shh. It's all right. It's all right. It's gone.

Boy   What was it, Papa?

Man   It was an earthquake.

EXT. ROAD – DAY

*Through swirls of soft ash and smoggy air, the **Man** appears
dressed as if homeless, a filthy old parka with the hood up, a
knapsack on his back, pushing a rusted shopping cart with a
bicycle mirror clamped to the handle and the blue tarp now
covering its load. The little **Boy**, similarly dressed with a
knapsack on his back, shuffles through the ash at his side, like
Depression-era dustbowl homeless.*

There is a flicker of lightning overhead, then more, but no thunder.

Man (*voice-over*)   The clocks stopped at one-seventeen
one morning. There was a long shear of bright light,
then a series of low concussions.

EXT. MOUNTAINSIDE, CRACKED ROAD – DAY

*Broken asphalt, the earthquake has caused a large fissure to
open up alongside the road with a sheer drop.*

*The **Man** and the **Boy** edge past burnt trees and shrubs.*

Man (*voice-over*)   Within a year there were fires on the
ridges and deranged chanting. The screams of the
murdered. By day the dead impaled on spikes along the
road.

EXT. LAKE – DAY

They trudge past a vast lake filled with dead trees.

Man (*voice-over*)   I think it's October but I can't be sure.
I haven't kept a calender for five years.

The Road

EXT. MOUNTAINSIDE – DAY

They truck along with the trolley through the fog, the ghostly shapes of dead trees on either side and the shapes of barren mountains in the background.

Man (*voice-over*)   Each day is more grey than the one before. Each night is darker – beyond darkness. The world gets colder week by week as the planet slowly dies. No animals have survived. All the crops are long gone.

EXT. EDGE OF WOODS – DAY

A tree falls behind them with a whump and they jump . . .

Man (*voice-over*)   Someday all the trees in the world will have fallen.

EXT. GAS STATION – DAY

*The **Man** forages for petrol, checking the nozzle of the pumps, rummaging through empty oilcans. He upends a bin to get at the empty oil bottles.*

*The **Boy** picks up a phone on a wall and listens to the dead earpiece.*

Man (*voice-over*)   The roads are peopled by refugees towing carts and road gangs carrying weapons, looking for fuel and food.

EXT. LONG ROAD – DAY

They head down a long straight road towards a dark, forbidding-looking tunnel – a turnpike.

Man (*voice-over*)   There has been cannibalism. Cannibalism is the great fear.

EXT. CITY – DAY

They emerge before a view of a deserted city-state . . .

EXT. MALL – DAY

They forage in a deserted mall.

There are skeletons and human bones here and there.

Man (*voice-over*)   Mostly I worry about food. Always food. Food and our shoes.

*Close-up – the **Boy** examines the head of a moose mounted on a wall in a Sears hunting store.*

Man (*voice-over*)   Sometimes I tell the boy old stories of courage and justice – difficult as they are to remember. All I know is, the child is my warrant and if he is not the word of God, then God never spoke.

End of credits/music.

EXT. RIDGE/CAMPSITE – EVENING

They are camped high up on the ridge of a mountainside. There is a camp fire with wet clothes hanging to dry on sticks beside it.

*The **Man** is erecting the tarp over string tied between two sticks stuck in the ground. The **Boy** is sitting lighting a lantern using the scavenged oil inside the makeshift tent, his shadow stark against the illuminated tarp.*

Boy   Now you can read me a story.

He gets out a book and looks at the pictures in the lamplight.

*The **Man** reads him a story . . .*

EXT. RIDGE/CAMPSITE – NIGHT

*The **Man** awakens bathed in fiery light as if the sun has come out. There is pale grey snow all around him with a quivering* *orange glow. He gets up to investigate, looks to the line of trees up the ridge where a forest fire is burning, crackling in the distance. He stands staring at the fire, the warmth and light moving him, enlivening him and not frightening him at all. The **Boy** has got up and appears at his side, yawning. He looks at the sky at a single grey snowflake drifting down.*

Boy   It's snowing!

Man   It's like it used to be when the sun came out.

*The **Boy** catches the snowflake in his hand, surprised.*

EXT. ROAD/PLAIN – DAY

They travel along the road through drifting wood smoke, smoke pouring off the ground like mist and thin black trees burning like candles on the snowy ridge.

They reach a spot where fire has crossed the road melting the tarmac. Their feet stick in the molten tarmac; it sucks at their shoes and they stop. Just ahead they see a set of footprints in the tar and study them.

Boy   Who is it?

Man   I don't know.

*The **Man** looks through a pair of binoculars and sees: a stooped figure up ahead, a **Dying Man** dragging one leg slightly, limping along. He stops and stands uncertainly, then continues. The **Boy** sees him too.*

Boy   What should we do, Papa?

Man   We're all right. Let's just follow and watch.

Boy   Take a look.

Man   Yeah. Take a look.

EXT. ROAD/HILL – LATE AFTERNOON

*The **Dying Man** is getting slower and slower as they climb a slope, following, until he finally stops and simply sits in the road.*

*The **Boy** hangs on to the **Man**'s coat anxiously as they approach.*

***Boy**'s point of view – the **Dying Man** is burnt, his clothing scorched and skin black with soot. One eye is burnt shut and his hair is a nitty wig of ash. His shoes are bound with wire and coated with road tar. As they pass by the **Dying Man** looks down, averting his eyes. The **Boy** keeps looking, unable to take his eyes off him.*

Boy   Papa, what's wrong with that man?

Man   He's been struck by lightning.

Boy   Can't we help him? Papa?

Man   No. We can't help him.

*They keep walking away and the **Boy** tugs at the **Man**'s coat.*

Boy   Papa?

Man   Stop it.

Boy   Can't we help him, Papa?

Man   No. We can't. There's nothing to be done for him.

EXT. BRIDGE – EVENING

*They are camped under the bridge; ash and slurry drift by on the river, a dull sulphur light from the fires glows against the sky. The **Boy** sits in silence with his back to the **Man**.*

Man   There's nothing we could have done. (*No reply.*) He's going to die. We can't share what we have or we'll die too.

Boy   I know.

Man   So when are you going to talk to me again?

Boy   I'm talking now.

Man   Are you sure?

Boy   Yes.

The Road

EXT. BARN – DAY

They come to a barn beside the road. They look at each other.

Man   Let's take a look.

The man picks up the revolver and they go inside cautiously.

INT. BARN – DAY

Three pairs of feet wearing different shoes – a man's shoes, a woman's shoes, and a child's sneakers – hang above three carefully placed chairs.

Man   Don't look.

*The **Boy** looks at the ground.*

You don't need to see this.

*The **Boy** takes a few steps, exploring; he eyes the empty hayloft but avoids looking at the hanged bodies.*

Boy   There could be something here. There could be corn or something.

Man   No, they ran out of food.

Boy   Maybe we could find some hayseeds in the hayloft?

*Now the **Boy** goes over to the swinging corpses, oddly curious.*

Man   It's not what you think. They committed suicide.

Boy   What does that mean?

Man   You know what that means.

*The **Man** goes outside while the **Boy** thinks about it a moment.*

EXT. FARM GATE – DAY

They walk away from the eerily silent farm, stopping at a gate by a weathered, paint-stripped letterbox.

Man   Come here.

10

*The **Boy** goes over and the **Man** takes out his revolver, opens the magazine and shows him: two bullets in the chamber.*

You see that? Two left. One for you and one for me.

*He places the **Boy**'s thumb on the hammer and cocks the pistol. He curls the **Boy**'s index finger around the trigger.*

You put it in your mouth and point it up. Like this. Just like I showed you.

*He puts the barrel of the pistol in his own mouth until the **Boy** nods, wide-eyed. He takes the pistol out of his mouth and uncocks it.*

You got it?

Boy   I think.

Man   Is it okay?

Boy   Okay.

*The **Man** puts the gun away and cuddles the **Boy** close. They set off again.*

INT. CLAPBOARD HOUSE – DAY

*Flashback – the **Woman** is sitting by the window, staring out at the garden, which is barren now, the sky grey but tinged with the same fireglow seen earlier; a film of grey ash covers dead lawn and shrubs, and inside the paintwork is grimy and colourless now, a lot of the furniture gone. A pile of broken-up furniture and pieces of the piano are stacked up next to the fireplace. In the fireplace the scorched, ashen remains of piano keys. The **Woman** is now heavily pregnant. The **Man** sets down chipped old plates and spoons, spoons beans from a pot and sits to eat.*

*As the **Woman** starts to eat she winces and freezes with a look of horror, spoon halfway to her mouth. She looks down and sees:*

Woman's *point of view – water and blood running down her legs.*

Woman   Oh no. Oh no.

Man   It's okay, I'll help you. Just like we said.

Woman   No no no . . .

Man   I'll heat water. We can do it.

As he goes out she moans in despair.

INT. KITCHEN/CLAPBOARD HOUSE – DAY

*The **Man** rushes in and opens a drawer in the sideboard.
Instead of cutlery it contains a pair of kitchen shears, a bottle of
antiseptic, worn but clean towels and a pair of worn-out yellow
rubber dishgloves, all laid out in readiness.*

*The **Woman** appears at the door, blood running down a leg.*

Woman   We don't have to.

Man   Well, I think we probably do.

Woman   What kind of life is this?

Man   It's life. It's the only thing left.

*He takes the **Woman** back into the other room.*

INT. DINING ROOM/CLAPBOARD HOUSE – DAY

*Terrible screaming. The **Woman** lies on the dining-room table,
screaming as she has her first contractions. The **Man** is wearing
the rubber gloves, one gloved hand resting on the **Woman**'s
leg, about to deliver his own baby. He wipes his brow and leaves
a smear of blood as the screaming goes on.*

Woman   I can't.

Man   It's coming.

End of flashback.

INT. TRAILER HOME – EVENING

*Inside a badly damaged trailer home, one wall half fallen off,
a pan of water boils on a small fire. The **Boy** sits shivering in
blankets as he eats beans from a tin, scraping around for the last*

*one or two. The **Man** opens his knapsack by the fire and produces a packet of cocoa. He fixes a cup of cocoa for the boy. He hands the **Boy** the cup of cocoa and as the **Boy** examines it and drinks, the **Man** surreptitiously pours himself a mug of water and sits blowing on it. The **Boy** realises the **Man** has left him all the cocoa.*

Boy   You promised not to do that.

Man   What?

Boy   You know what, Papa. I have to watch you all the time.

Man   I know, I'm sorry.

Boy   If you break little promises you'll break big ones. That's what you said.

*The **Man** relents, pouring the hot water back into the pan and taking some of the **Boy**'s cocoa into his own cup. The **Boy** wipes his finger around the inside of the empty bean tin and licks his finger.*

Man   Watch your finger.

Boy   You always say that.

Man   That's because you always do it.

*The **Man** spreads bits of a worn-out road map on the boards and studies them.*

Boy   What are you doing?

Man   We have to keep moving. We have to go south to the coast.

Boy   Why?

Man   It'll be better at the coast.

Boy   Why?

Man   Because we're going to freeze here.

He picks up the map pieces carefully.

The Road

*The **Man** and the **Boy** truck along the blacktop.*

*At the crest of a hill they come to faded billboards advertising motels and stop. The **Boy** notices a sign in the distance, which has words painted over a faded advertisement: odd, nonsensical, Biblical ramblings about 'bones' and 'the dead'. The **Man** follows the **Boy**'s gaze and reads 'Behold the valley of slaughter – Jeremiah 19:6'.*

Man Do you remember your alphabet?

Boy Yes.

Man Can you read that?

Boy (*scrutinising it*) No.

Man Good, let's go.

*The **Man** takes out the revolver, cocks it in readiness and places it on the tarp as they move. The **Boy** eyes the **Man** nervously, eyes the gun, and they move off.*

EXT. TURNPIKE, TUNNEL APPROACH – DAY

*They trudge along the turnpike towards the opening of a large tunnel and the **Boy** suddenly comes to a stop, increasingly upset, unable to face continuing into the black mouth of the tunnel.*

Boy I can't, I just can't.

Man There's no other way.

Boy We could go over.

Man We can't take the cart over.

Boy We don't know what's in there.

Man There's nothing in there. It's just the same as it is out here. Okay?

Boy (*beat; very reluctant*) Okay.

*The boy sticks close to the **Man**'s side. The man has the revolver in his belt now and his parka unzipped ready, as they nervously walk towards the mouth of the tunnel.*

INT. TUNNEL – DAY

*The **Man** has his arm around the boy as they push the cart cautiously ahead, acutely aware of all that's around them. They pass footprints in the dried sludge on the ground. Ash and litter blowing about and a handful of mummified dead refugees appear along the sides of the tunnel, sitting and lying on camp stretchers, their bags and supplies long since looted. They are shrivelled and drawn like latter-day bogfolk, shoeless: a couple of men, a woman, a small child and a dog.*

*The **Man** stares at the group.*

*The **Boy** stares at the small child and then at the mummified dog, transfixed. The **Man** puts out his hand for the **Boy** to take. The **Boy** takes his hand and the **Man** moves him on.*

Man   Just remember that the things you put into your head are for ever.

Boy   But you forget some things, don't you?

Man   You forget what you want to remember and you remember what you want to forget.

EXT. TUNNEL EXIT AND TURNPIKE – EARLY MORNING

*The **Man** and the **Boy** are asleep inside an abandoned car amongst a line of other abandoned vehicles littering the turnpike.*

INT. ABANDONED CAR – EARLY MORNING

*Now the **Boy**'s hand rests on the **Man**'s chest as he sleeps. The **Man** breathes stertorously, wheezing a little, and the **Boy**'s small hand goes up and down on his chest.*

*Suddenly the **Man** wakes and rolls on to his side, listening, the revolver lying beside him. He slips his hand on to the revolver and raises his head slowly. He looks around – nothing but the sound of a distant diesel engine. He looks at the **Boy** fast asleep. When he looks back at the tunnel he sees a nightmarish vision:*

Man's *point of view – exiting the tunnel, shuffling through the ash, a group of hooded men, some in gas masks and filthy bio-hazard suits, slouching along, coughing, casting their heads from side to side and swinging clubs and lengths of pipe – a road gang. The **Man** listens to the sound of a diesel truck behind the gang.*

Man   Quickly. Quick . . .

*The **Boy** jolts awake as the **Man** shoves his pistol in his belt, grabs the boy by the hand. They slide out of the car and crouch on the ground, the **Boy** is frozen with fear.*

It's all right. It's all right, but we have to run. Don't look back. Come on.

Their backpacks are still left in the back of the car . . .

Man   Run . . . run . . .

*The flatbed truck rumbles into view, **Men** from the gang standing on the flatbed looking around, some holding rifles. The **Boy** falls and the **Man** pulls him to his feet with such force he lifts him clean off the ground and has to dangle him back down again.*

Man   You okay? It's all right . . . Come on . . .

They rush down the embankment into the trees alongside the turnpike.

EXT. TURNPIKE UNDERPASS – DAY

They run through the woods. The truck is heard in the background, the motor missing and sputtering, coils of black diesel smoke coiling through the woods. The motor dies with a flapping rattle and there's silence.

*The **Man** and the **Boy** crouch in frozen silence, the truck now on the overpass nearby, dangerously exposed to the view of the gang. They listen to the gang talking and raising the hood of the truck.*

*The **Man** puts his arm around the **Boy** and draws his pistol as they see the truck begin to roll, the gang pushing it . . . but it coughs and stalls again.*

*The **Man** sees a **Gang Member** coming down the embankment, unbuckling his belt. He is emaciated, in dirty blue overalls and a gas company cap, and has a long beard cut square at the bottom and a bad tattoo of a bird on his neck. He doesn't stop, just keeps coming, closer and closer until he's just feet away, almost on top of them. He unzips his pants and takes a piss. As he stands pissing his eyes roam around – at any moment he could look to the side and see them crouching there.*

*The **Man** is wide-eyed, gun ready, eyes darting from the **Gang Member** to the **Boy** to the gun. The **Gang Member** rolls his shoulders and exercises his neck . . . He looks down and studies the steam coming off his piss.*

*The **Man** silently trains his pistol at the head of the **Gang Member** who, as if by instinct, rolls his head around and looks right at him.*

Man   Just keep it coming.

*The **Gang Member** sees the gun and stops pissing, looks back at the truck, zips his fly.*

Man   Don't look at them. Look at me. If you call out you're dead. Where you from?

Gang Member   Does it matter? Where you from?

Man   What's the truck running on?

Gang Member   Diesel fuel.

Man   Where d'you get that?

Gang Member   I don't know.

Man   You don't know, huh?

The Road

The **Gang Member** *just stares, not answering.*

You got ammunition for those rifles?

The **Gang Member** *looks back towards the truck.*

Man I told you not to look back there. Where d'you get all that stuff?

Gang Member Found it.

Man What are you eating?

Gang Member Whatever we can find.

Man Whatever you can find, huh?

Gang Member Yeah . . .

Now the **Gang Member** *looks at the* **Boy***, causing the* **Man** *to raise the revolver and cock it.*

Gang Member*'s point of view – he is looking down the barrel at the magazine and sees empty space.*

Gang Member You won't shoot that thing. You ain't got but two shells. Maybe just one. And they'll hear the shot.

On the overpass the road gang are looking around, murmuring as they notice one of their number missing.

Man Maybe. But you won't. It'll be through your skull and inside your brain before you can hear it.

The **Man** *steps closer and aims the gun at the* **Gang Member***'s forehead, hammer back, ready.*

To hear it you'll need a frontal lobe and things with names like *colliculus* and *temporal gyrus* and you won't have them any more because they'll just be soup.

Gang Member Are you a doctor?

Man I'm not anything any more.

Gang Member We got a hurt man. It'd be worth your while.

The **Man** *glances in the direction of the road gang, then back at the* **Gang Member***, who is still eyeing the* **Boy***. The* **Boy** *is* *sitting with his hands on top of his head, peeking out through his arms, terrified as the tension escalates.*

Man   If you look at him again I'll shoot you in the head.

Gang Member   I'll bet that boy is hungry. Why don't you all just come on to the truck? Get something to eat. Ain't no need to be such a hard ass.

Man   You don't have anything to eat. Let's go.

Gang Member   I ain't going nowheres.

Man   You think I won't kill you, but you're wrong.

Gang Member   You know what I think? I think you're chickenshit. You never killed a man in your life.

*He drops his belt on the ground with a clatter, a canteen and army pouch hanging from it. The **Man** eyes the army pouch, eyes the gang on the road – and notices for the first time some of them are wearing the same army pouches. One is banging his stick on the side of the truck to call their lost member. The **Man** is distracted by this and when he looks up the **Gang Member** has taken two silent steps and is standing between him and the **Boy**, holding a knife.*

Man   What do you think you're going to do with that?

*Without a word the **Gang Member** dives and grabs the **Boy**, rolls and lands on his feet holding the **Boy** against his chest with his knife at his throat. Simultaneously the **Man** drops to his knees, trains the pistol and fires from six feet away, shooting the **Gang Member** in the forehead. He falls back and lies with blood bubbling from the wound, eyes open, the **Boy** lying in his lap in shock, deafened, expressionless, covered with gore and mute as a stone.*

*The gang hear the loud shot and freeze; they start looking around them more urgently now. The **Man** grabs the dazed **Boy** by the hand and yells, but in his deafness the **Boy** hears only a muted soup of words:*

Man (*muted*)   Move! Let's go!

The **Man** *shoves the pistol in his belt, hoists the* **Boy** *on to his shoulders and sets off down the road at a run.*

EXT. WOODS – DAY

They crash through the woods, the **Man** *straining to keep the* **Boy** *aloft and find a path through the trees – the* **Boy** *clutching the* **Man**'s *head with both hands.*

There's a sickening thud and the **Man** *falls, the* **Boy** *flying off with a cry. The* **Man** *struggles to gather his wits, unsure whether he's been felled by another man.*

Man (*muted*)   Come on. Get up, get up quickly!

The **Man** *swings the* **Boy** *on to his shoulders and runs.*

EXT. WOODS / TURNPIKE – DAY

The **Man** *and* **Boy** *stagger through trees and the man drops to his knees, letting the* **Boy** *down. They are back by the turnpike again. They listen and watch, utterly exhausted and out of breath. The* **Man** *is wheezing, the* **Boy** *at his side, holding his hand, staring, in shock still.*

Man   Shh. It's okay now. You're going to be okay.

Boy's *point of view – the* **Boy** *can still hear nothing, temporarily deaf. But he sees the* **Man** *talking and looking around, through 360 degrees, trying to work out where it's safe to go.*

Man   Come on.

He grabs the **Boy**'s *hand and they take off again.*

EXT. WOODS – EVENING

The **Boy** *sits staring, shocked, as the* **Man** *tries to wipe the blood and gore from his face but it's thick and congealed now. His hands tremble as he tries to pick it from the* **Boy**'s *hair.*

Man   It's okay . . . it's okay now . . .

Frightened by the **Boy**'s *muteness, he unzips his parka and holds him close under the parka.*

The **Man** *picks up his revolver, checks the chamber; only one bullet left. He eyes the flickering shadows in the distance and then eyes the* **Boy**, *making minute calculations of distance, calibrating the space between the road gang and the* **Boy**. *He holds the revolver up and cocks it.*

Man (*voice-over*)   I try to look like any common travelling killer but my heart is hammering. When it comes to the boy I have only one question: can you do it? When the time comes?

There is no moon, but not far away, perhaps thirty yards, a fiery torch makes its way through the woods. About fifty yards away from that another torch is being used to search . . . shadows flicker ominously. The sounds of twigs snapping underfoot and branches being broken as the road gang searches wordlessly, just breathing heavily through their masks and beards. The **Man** *clutches the* **Boy** *tighter, and stifles a cough.*

They remain frozen like this, unable to budge.

Fade out.

EXT. EMBANKMENT — DAWN

They are by a thin, toxic red stream, slushy ice at the edges and pink froth. The **Man** *leans down and pushes ice away and scoops up a handful of grey water. He runs it through the boy's hair to wash it and the* **Boy** *flinches with cold. He rubs more icy water into the* **Boy**'s *hair, roughly, quickly, with a sense of panic as he helplessly tries to wash out lumps of flesh and blood. The* **Boy** *is weeping silently and shivering from the extreme cold as the* **Man** *picks out the dried gore and washes the hair clean.*

Man   It's no use crying. You have to talk to me.

He dries the **Boy**'s *hair with his hat as he talks.*

Man   I'm not going to let anything happen to you . . .
I'm going to take care of you . . . I'm always going to try
and be here for you . . . and I'm going to kill anybody
who touches you.

*He smooths the **Boy**'s hair down with shaking fingers, clumsily
trying to brush it out of his eyes, a fatherly instinct to make the
Boy neat.*

Man   Because that's my job. Do you understand?

*When he's through the **Man** lifts the **Boy**'s thin arms, puts a vest
over his head, then a ragged sweater, then he folds the **Boy** into his
parka, zips it up to the neck and kisses him on the top of the head.*

Man   Come on, we need to get the cart back.

EXT. EMBANKMENT BY TUNNEL EXIT – DAY

*Approaching the embankment, the **Man** walks quickly and
stealthily, wired, listening to the silence, straining to hear, sure he's
being watched. The **Boy** stumbles along behind, slower, fatigued,
making the **Man** anxious. The **Man** leaves the boy hiding.*

Man (*whispers*)   Wait here.

*He starts to climb the embankment and hears little running
footsteps as the **Boy** comes after him; he turns to face the **Boy**
urgently, exasperated.*

Man (*whispers*)   No, I need you to wait. I'll hear you if
you call. I'll just be a little ways and I'll be able to hear
you if you get scared and you call me and I'll come right
away.

*He walks off but hears . . . the little **Boy**'s footsteps running
after him again – he turns around.*

I said wait!

*The **Boy**'s face crinkles up and a tear rolls down.*

Stop it. I need you to do what I say. Take the gun.

*The **Boy** freezes, refusing to take the gun.*

Just take it will you?

The **Boy** *shakes his head.*

We don't have time for this. We need our food. What's left.

The **Man** *shoves the gun into the* **Boy**'s *hand.*

Don't argue.

He creeps up the embankment. The **Boy** *just stares at the revolver.*

EXT. TURNPIKE ROAD – DAY

The **Man** *searches for the cart. He comes to where they'd left it in between the abandoned cars. Their backpacks lie open on the ground, next to the cart on its side, its contents spilled out, mostly plundered, just a few children's books and toys, old pots and pans, shoes and ragged clothing remaining. Nearby are the remains of a large campfire in the middle of the turnpike. The man collects up the few remaining possessions and puts them into the backpacks.*

Man's *point of view – he sees charred billets of wood, ash and . . . the bones of the shot* **Gang Member**. *Nearby is a pool of his blood and guts, still gently steaming. He nudges the bones with the toe of his shoe.*

EXT. EMBANKMENT BY THE TURNPIKE – DAY

Below, down the embankment the **Boy** *is waiting obediently with the gun.*

The **Man** *heads back to the* **Boy**, *trying to think what to say. The* **Boy** *hands the gun back and takes the* **Man**'s *hand and they walk away into the woods, the* **Man** *tucking the gun back into his belt.*

Man Let's get out of here. The freeway's too dangerous. Find the back roads.

Boy Okay.

The Road

*Flashback – now the house is in considerable disrepair, no furniture, the skirting boards falling away, large cracks in the walls, cornices and lamp fittings pulling away from the ceilings, water marks from rain, the windows covered with corrugated-iron sheets. The **Man** and the **Woman** are sitting across from each other with a lamp illuminating the dark. Between them lies the revolver seen earlier. The **Woman** picks up the gun and swings open the magazine. There are two bullets in it; she takes them out and places them on the table, one after the other.*

Woman   That's all that's left. I should have done it when there were more bullets in the gun.

*The **Man** shuts his eyes, unable to take it. In the corner, the **Boy** is standing in the background, drawing on the walls.*

Sooner or later – no, listen – they will catch up with us and they will kill us. They will rape me –

Man   No –

Woman   And they will rape him –

Man   Please no – just – no –

Woman   They are going to rape us and kill us and eat us and you won't face it. You'd rather wait for it to happen.

Man   Please.

Woman   Stop it.

Man   I'll do anything.

Woman   Such as what?

She picks up the revolver and puts the two bullets into the chamber.

I thought about not even telling you. Just doing it. I'd empty every godamn bullet into my brain and leave you with nothing.

Man   Don't say that. Don't talk this way.

Woman   There's nothing left to talk about . . . My heart was ripped out of me the night he was born . . .

Man   Please don't do this. I won't let anything happen. We'll survive.

Woman   I don't want to survive! I'd take him with me if it weren't for you. You know I would. Why can't you face it?

Man   Will you listen? You're talking crazy –

Woman   It's not crazy and you know it. It's the right thing to do.

They glance at the **Boy**.

Other families do it.

She goes to the **Boy**, *strokes his hair, kisses him, makes a reassuring display of being motherly.*

Time for bed, there's a good boy.

She picks him up in her arms and carries him off to bed. End of flashback.

EXT. RAVINE/WATERFALL – DAY

The thunder of a waterfall. The river disappears into space. The **Boy** *and the* **Man** *stand staring up at the waterfall, eighty feet above, shrouded in grey mist. A colour spectrum is visible rising from the waterfall, like a rainbow – the boy is transfixed, clutching the* **Man***'s arm for safety.*

Boy   What is it?

The **Man** *looks at the* **Boy**, *surprised he's talking again.*

Man   It's a waterfall.

Boy   Look. Colours.

Man   There used to be colour everywhere. You don't remember. It was before you were born.

The Road

*The **Boy** approaches the water's edge, shallow and clear with gravel and pebbles sparkling at the bottom. He scoops up some water, surprised that it seems clean.*

Boy   Look. It's clear.

Man   Do you want to go in?

Boy   I don't know.

Man   Sure you do.

Boy   Is it okay?

Man   Just don't swallow any.

*The **Man** unzips his parka and slips it to the ground. The **Boy** eyes the **Man**, surprised – then does the same.*

EXT. RIVER/WATERFALL – DAY

*Naked, pale, filthy dirty and shivering with cold, the **Boy** frolics in the spray of the waterfall. The **Man** watches him enjoying himself by the waterfall, clutching his shoulders, hopping up and down. He joins him.*

EXT. RAVINE/ROCKFACE – EVENING

*The **Man** meticulously filters water through a rag into a pan. In the background, the waterfall can be heard rumbling. The **Boy** has painted his face with crayons, drawing a bizarre set of fangs and dripping blood around his mouth. The **Man** studies the **Boy**'s painted face a moment.*

Man   Listen. That man back there . . . There's not many good guys left, that's all. We have to watch out for the bad guys. And we have to talk. Always. We have to just . . . you know . . . keep carrying the fire . . .

Boy   What fire?

Man   The fire inside you.

*The **Boy** is thoughtful a minute, and then:*

Boy   Are we still the good guys?

Man   Yes. We're still the good guys.

Boy   And we always will be, no matter what happens?

The **Man** *eyes the* **Boy** *uncertainly, unsure if he can promise this.*

Man   Always will be. Yeah.

The **Man** *goes back to filtering the water.*

EXT. THE RIVER/VALLEY – MORNING

The **Man** *and the* **Boy** *are trudging along, away from the waterfall now.*

Man   We have to keep moving. Other people might be attracted to the waterfall just like we were. We wouldn't hear them coming.

They stop to look at a lake surrounded by fog down in the valley.

Boy   Do you think there could be fish in the lake?

Man   No. There's nothing in the lake.

They move on.

EXT. BACK ROAD – DAY

They come around a bend in the road and immediately hear the roar of river rapids. Up ahead they see a bridge with a jackknifed truck on it.

EXT. BRIDGE – DAY

They walk out on to the bridge over grey frothing water and inspect the truck. The tyres are flat, the cab jammed against the railings. The trailer end has swung across the road, knocked out the railings and lies with its last few feet hanging over the side of the bridge, blocking the bridge off completely.

27

The Road

EXT. ABANDONED TRUCK – DAY

*The **Man** climbs up on to the gas tanks, wipes the glass and peers into the cab. He swings the door open and climbs inside, pulling the door shut behind.*

INT. TRUCK/CAB – DAY

He looks around at discarded detritus, old magazines and trash. He checks behind the seats where there is a mattress on a bunk and calls out.

Man Come up here.

INT. TRUCK/CAB – NIGHT

Snow continues to fall on the dusty windscreen. Outside, all around, snow falls, silently, covering the truck and the bridge, transforming it. They are both still awake, unable to sleep, staring at the transformed world, carpeted by snow.

Boy I'm hungry.

Man I know. So am I.

Boy Can I ask you something?

Man Of course.

Boy Are we going to die?

Man No. Sometime. Not now.

Boy And we're still going south?

Man Yes.

Boy So we'll be warm?

Man Yes.

Boy And there might be food there?

Man Everything depends on reaching the coast.

Boy Okay.

*The **Man** draws a blanket around him and kisses the **Boy** goodnight. It is now pitch black.*

Man   Go to sleep.

Boy   I wish I was with my mom.

They are silent a moment, until:

Man   You mean you wish you were dead.

Boy   Yeah.

Man   You mustn't say that. It's a bad thing to say.

Boy   I can't help it.

Man   I know, but you have to. You have to stop thinking about her. We both do.

Boy   How do I do that?

*The **Man** is silent, lost in thought.*

EXT. TRUCK/CAB – EARLY HOURS

*The **Man** gets down from the cab and walks a few feet in the dark and snow. He coughs a bit, takes a few breaths of air, and walks away from the truck, vanishing into the mist.*

EXT. CAMP/ROAD – EARLY HOURS

*The **Man** is alone now by the road. He takes out his wallet and sifts through: money, ancient cards, driver's licence and a picture of himself and the **Woman** on their wedding day, which he studies a moment sadly.*

Man (*voice-over*)   She was gone, and the coldness of it was her final gift . . . She died somewhere in the dark . . . There is no other tale to tell.

He lays everything out on the grey slushy ground, then flings the wallet into the river and walks back to camp, leaving the photo and cards to blow away.

The Road

EXT. CLAPBOARD HOUSE/YARD – NIGHT

Flashback – the **Woman** *kisses the* **Man**.

Man Will you tell him goodbye?

Woman No. I won't. I can't.

Man Will you at least wait till morning? Stay with me through the night?

Woman No. I have to go now.

They kiss again, she turns and walks away out of the yard.

Man What am I going to tell him? What are we going to do without you?

Woman You should move south. You won't survive another winter here.

The **Man** *follows a few steps and she stops and turns to him.*

Man Why won't you help me?

Woman I can't help you. Don't you understand? This is how I'm helping you.

Man Where are you going to go? You can't even see.

Woman I don't need to see.

Man I'm begging you.

Woman Please don't. Please.

The **Man** *stares. She goes, vanishing into the darkness.*

End of flashback.

EXT. CITY LIMITS – DUSK

The **Man** *stares. In the distance, a dead city.*

EXT. OVERPASS/CITY LIMITS – EVENING

The **Man** *and the* **Boy** *approach the edge of the city. Up ahead a cluster of three tall buildings, a dozen or so floors of concrete* *and glass, the upper floors of one illuminated by the flickering fire glow of candlelight inside. The **Man** stops and stares and the **Boy** follows his gaze.*

In one of the illuminated windows a silhouetted figure stares back at them, somebody in the building. In another window another silhouetted figure is staring out, motionless; they could be refugees, cannibals or more mummified dead for all we know.

Boy   Who are they, Papa?

Man   I don't know.

Boy   What if it's more bad guys?

Man   It won't be more bad guys. Don't worry. Stay close.

He takes hold of the gun and they walk in a different direction now, giving the high rises a wide berth.

Man   Keep low. We'll be okay.

*When they get to the end of the block they stop and the **Man** checks around the corner before they cross the street. In the distance three men appear, emaciated, slow moving. They step forward, stop and watch the **Boy** and the **Man**.*

EXT. OUTSKIRTS/CITY – DAY

*The **Man**, now carrying the revolver, and the **Boy** head off down a railway track that leads away from the city.*

EXT. COUNTRY RAILWAY LINE – DAY

*In the country, along the railway, they see past a small road to a once grand house on a rise. It is tall and stately with white Doric columns across the front and a gravel drive that curves up from the road through a field of dead, foot-long grass. They stand there staring at it, the **Boy** still holding the **Man**'s hand. The **Man** listens – nothing but the wind in the dead bracken, a creak of a door or shutter rattling.*

Man   I think we should take a look.

The Road

Boy   I'm scared.

Man   There's nothing to be scared of.

EXT. DRIVEWAY/STATELY HOME – DAY

*The **Man** sets off up the drive. He stops and faces the **Boy** who is rooted to the spot.*

Man   You want to stay here?

Boy   No.

*The **Boy** joins him and they set off slowly up the drive, through patches of melting snow. There is a tall, dead privet fence with a deserted birds' nest in it.*

EXT. PORCH/STATELY HOME – DAY

*They climb the steps to the porch, the **Boy** clutching the **Man**'s hand. They notice a window is slightly open. The man goes to it, opens the window wide, looks inside.*

INT. FOYER/STATELY HOME – DAY

*They climb through the window on to black-and-white marble tiles, and the **Man** carefully shuts the window a little so it's the same as when he found it. They regard the room. Binoculars set up on a tripod sit next to an arm chair. An elaborate staircase in front of them, William Morris wallpaper, water-stained and sagging, plaster mouldings and cornices sagging from the ceiling. The **Man** takes the binoculars.*

They cross back to the other side, where there is a great hall of a drawing room, high ceilings, huge fireplace with raw brick around it where the wood has been stripped, a pile of warm-weather clothing, boots and backpacks on the floor by the hearth.

Boy   Papa?

Man   Shh.

INT. KITCHEN/STATELY HOME – DAY

They creep in and find blackened pots and pans, a cord with a bell for servants, trash piled on the floor and worktops, a rusted sink covered in mould, bare cupboards. In the floor is a hatch with a lock set in a steel plate. The man examines it while the **Boy** *tugs at his arm, frightened.*

Boy Papa, let's go.

Man There's a reason this is locked.

The **Boy** *is now panicky, hopping about, close to tears.*

Boy Don't open it – don't!

Man I need something to pry it open.

Boy No!

The **Man** *goes out abruptly and the* **Boy** *follows, wringing his hands in fear.*

EXT. BACK GARDEN/STATELY HOME – DAY

The **Man** *comes out the back door with his revolver drawn, looks around and sees an old station wagon with flat tyres on the dead grass. Beside it is a forty-gallon cauldron on the blackened remnants of a fire. There is also a wooden smoke house with thin wisps of smoke coming off it. The* **Man** *studies it nervously, sniffing the air, then goes to the toolshed and starts sorting through tools. He finds a long-handled spade and hefts it in his hands.*

INT. KITCHEN/STATELY HOME – DAY

The spade chops into the wood around the lock on the hatch. The **Man** *hacks away, then prises up the hatch, lock and all, revealing a gap of darkness.*

Boy Papa . . .

Man   Listen to me. Just stop it. We're starving. Do you understand? I have to do this. I don't have any choice.

*The **Man** opens the hatch fully and lays it on the floor.*

Man   Just wait here.

Boy   I'm going with you.

Man   Okay. Just stay close to me. Nothing's going to happen.

They descend the rough wooden steps.

INT. CELLAR/STATELY HOME – DAY

*There is a terrible stench and they have to cover their mouths and noses with their parkas. The **Man** gets out his lighter, lights it and tries to light the way.*

***Man**'s point of view – blackness, except the small area illuminated by the lighter as the **Man** searches: part of a stone wall; then a clay floor; an old mattress with dark stains. The glow of the flame crawls across the floor to a corner as the **Man** steps closer, then plays the lighter along from the corner to reveal:*

*Huddled against the wall, all trying to hide, shielding their shining eyes from the light, naked **Men** and **Women**, thin as skeletons like inmates in a death camp. The **Boy** jumps, shocked, and the **Man** freezes, staring, struck dumb by:*

*On a mattress on the floor, a **Naked Man** with his legs gone to the hip, their stumps blackened and burned, cauterised. The **Boy** covers his eyes.*

Man   Jesus . . .

*The **Man on the Mattress** turns to them and whispers, a low indistinct murmur at first.*

Man on Mattress   Help us . . . please help us . . .

Man   Christ . . . Oh Christ . . .

34

*The others join in, an eerie chorus of whispering, 'Help us . . .
Please help us . . .' The* **Man** *turns and grabs the* **Boy** *and
rushes for the steps.*

Hurry . . . Go . . . Move!

The **Man** *drops the lighter as he tries to push the* **Boy** *up the
steps. Out of nowhere a* **Bearded Face** *appears at the foot of
the stairs, blinking.*

Bearded Face   Please . . . they're taking us to the
smoke house.

The **Bearded Face** *reaches out and feebly tries to grab the*
Man's *arm but he breaks free and concentrates on getting the*
Boy *up the steps, following in a blind panic, fumbling and
missing his footing.*

Man   Hurry – hurry!

They scramble up the steps towards the light of the hatch as the
Bearded Face *reaches out and tries one last time to grab at
the* **Man**'s *feet, but he kicks free.*

INT. KITCHEN/STATELY HOME – DAY

The **Man** *scrambles out, slams the door shut and drags a solid
table over the door. He looks around for the* **Boy***.*

Man   Christ. Run!

The **Boy** *is near the window, dancing up and down in terror,
pointing out the window to:*

EXT. FIELDS – DAY

Coming up the path towards the house are four **Bearded
Men** *and two* **Women***, all suspiciously well-fed and
healthy-looking. One of the* **Bearded Men** *holds hands
with one of the* **Women***, as if they were returning from a
stroll before dinner.*

The Road

INT. KITCHEN/STATELY HOME – DAY

The **Man** *stares a moment, frozen with horror, then grabs the* **Boy** *by the hand and jerks him away.*

Man   Run. Run!

INT. FOYER/STATELY HOME – DAY

They tear through to the front door; the **Man** *fumbles to get it open, but it has a well-maintained deadlock on it. He stares out the window next to the door and sees:*

Man's *point of view – the* **Well-Fed People** *are climbing the steps of the porch. The* **Man** *grabs the* **Boy** *and they rush through into the kitchen.*

INT. KITCHEN/STATELY HOME – DAY

In the kitchen the hatch is being lifted from underneath and the table elevating inches. They rush back out again.

INT. FOYER/STATELY HOME – DAY

As they reach the stairs, a key turns in the lock and the **Man** *picks up the* **Boy** *in his arms and they sprint to a door under the stairs. As they get through the door the front door swings open and the* **Well-Fed People** *drift inside.*

INT. REST ROOM – DAY

They are in a small rest room under the stairs, just a toilet and a basin. The **Boy**'s *face is level with the basin and while the* **Man** *is holding the door shut the* **Boy** *comes face to face with the contents of the basin:*

Boy's *point of view – bloodstained clothing soaking in bloody water and tallow in the basin. Around the basin are bloody red hand prints on the white porcelain.*

Man's *point of view – through a thin crack he sees the*
Well-Fed People *on the far side of the foyer, chatting*
casually. He is not close enough to hear everything they say, but
close enough to see that the men's beards are trimmed and they
wear well-repaired clothes.

Well-Fed Woman   I'm going to freshen up.

Bearded Man   I need a drink.

Well-Fed Woman 2   I'm going up to change.

He hears one of the **Women** *stomping across the old*
floorboards and up the stairs to change while the other **Woman**
takes a few steps towards the rest room, then turns back towards
the window as the conversation lurches on.

Bearded Man 2   Who left this window open?

Well-Fed Woman   I leave it open for the smell.

Bearded Man 2   What smell?

Well-Fed Woman   You don't smell it any more?

Bearded Man   Who wants a drink?

They hear the sound of the window being closed and latched. As
all this goes on, the **Man** *is frozen, eyes wide with fear; he slips*
the pistol from his belt, cocks it and squats on his haunches so
he's close to the **Boy***, desperate, unable to decide what to do,*
unable to think straight with fear.

The **Boy** *is staring from the door to the pistol to the bloodied*
basin as if hypnotised, in shock, babbling somewhat.

Boy (*mumbling, to self*)   Bad guys . . . bad men . . .

Man   Shh, shh . . .

There are footsteps outside the door as the **Well-Fed People**
drift closer and then away again. The **Man** *starts to cough*
but he has the revolver in one hand and the boy's hand in his
other. The **Man** *tries to stifle his cough but can't. Then the*
Boy *notices and holds his own small hand to the* **Man**'s
mouth, stifling his coughing as the talk goes on outside:

Well-Fed Woman   Will you help me with the dirty dishes?

Bearded Man 2   I'm hungry.

As the coughing subsides a little the **Man** *takes the* **Boy**'s *hand from his mouth and pushes the revolver into it.*

Man   Take it.

The **Boy** *tries to resist, shaking his head, terrified, mute.*

Man (*whispers*)   Take it.

The **Man** *puts his left arm around the* **Boy**'s *tiny, thin shoulders and holds him close.*

Man (*whispers*)   Don't be afraid. If they get hold of you, you're going to have to do it just like everybody else. Do you understand? Shh. No crying. Do you hear me?

The **Woman** *turns from the window and one of the* **Bearded Men** *pours whisky and hands her a glass.*

The **Boy** *is weeping and shaking his head as the* **Man** *shows him again what to do with the gun.*

Man (*whispers*)   Stop crying. You have to be a brave boy. You know how to do it.

Boy (*whispers*)   I think so.

Man (*whispers*)   Say 'Yes I do, Papa.'

He stares down at the little **Boy** *who just holds the gun feebly . . . He realises the* **Boy** *won't use it. After a moment of tortuous contemplation, the* **Man** *very gently takes the gun from the* **Boy**'s *hand and the* **Boy** *sits forlornly, staring down at his hands, afraid to look at the* **Man** *now. When the* **Boy** *looks up again he is staring down the barrel of the pistol, the* **Man** *aiming the large revolver at the* **Boy**'s *forehead.*

Boy   What are you doing?

The **Man**'s *hand shakes, his thumb trembles on the hammer as he cocks it . . .*

Papa?

Man   I'm sorry. I'm so sorry.

Boy   Will I see you again? When will I see you?

*The **Man**'s finger trembles on the trigger as he slowly squeezes it . . . At that moment there's a loud thump from the kitchen and the **Well-Fed People** stop and listen, then rush through to the kitchen, and immediately there's a commotion as they see the state of the hatch with the table over it.*

Bearded Man 2 (*out of vision*)   What the fuck do you think you're doing? Huh? What the fuck do you think you're doing . . . ?

Well-Fed Woman (*out of vision*)   Don't look at me like that. What are you doing?

*The **Man** gathers his wits and opens the door a crack.*

Man   Follow me, take my hand, don't let go.

INT. FOYER/STATELY HOME – DAY

*The **Man** bursts out of the rest room with the **Boy** and they make a dash for the window. He sticks his gun in his belt and wrestles with the window, an old colonial-style frame which sticks.*

*From behind the closed kitchen door they hear muffled grunts and shouts until the **Man** wrenches the window open, stuffs the **Boy** through and follows.*

EXT. PORCH/STATELY HOME – DAY

*The **Man** picks the **Boy** up and they rush down the steps.*

EXT. DRIVEWAY/STATELY HOME – DAY

*They rush down the driveway and the **Man** drags the **Boy** through a gap in the dead privet hedge on to the road.*

The Road

They hesitate a moment on the road, deciding.

Man   Come on, keep running!

They rush across the road to the woods on the other side, the
***Boy** ahead as the **Man** checks behind them. The **Man** looks*
*back towards the house; two of the **Well-Fed People** have*
come outside, looking around suspiciously. He hits the ground
*and takes the **Boy** with him; they lie flat at the edge of the*
woods and the road. They are wildly out of breath, chests
*heaving, the **Man** coughing. The **Man** looks up and notices a*
children's tree house facing the road, another tripod and a chair
perched inside of it.

Man   Keep your head down.

***Man**'s point of view – the **Well-Fed People** walk a few steps*
*down the drive and a **Bearded Man** looks through a black-*
plastic hand-held telescope. He scans the road and the woods, but
*not directly at the **Man** and the **Boy** hiding. The **Well-Fed***
***People** start looking around the side of the house, walking away.*
*The **Man** and the **Boy** get up, dash through the treeline and*
disappear into the woods.

EXT. WOODS – NIGHT

A dull moon hidden in the ashen sky and the outlines of trees
as they set off through the woods, sleepy, stumbling like drunks
now. They hear a hideous shriek in the distance, coming from the
house. They stop, hearing another shriek and a man's screaming.
*The **Man** holds the **Boy** close and tries to cover the **Boy**'s ears*
as they stare and wait for it to pass.

Man   We'll be safe soon.

Boy   They're going to eat those people, aren't they,
Papa?

*The **Man** does not answer. They walk on.*

EXT. SEARS DEPARTMENT STORE/SHOPPING MALL – NIGHT

They are back in the outskirts of the city, trudging through the parking lot of a huge shopping mall, just outside what used to be Sears department store. A dull moon hidden in the ashen sky illuminates the ruined store front as the **Man** *looks up at the mall, thinking. The* **Boy** *is just staring into space, still in shock.*

INT. SEARS/MALL – NIGHT

The **Man** *and the* **Boy** *have set up camp in the mall, outside the Sears entrance. The* **Man** *is building a big fire. The* **Boy** *stares through the glass at the deserted department store. Nearby, strewn across the doorway are bunches and bundles of cash in notes and coins . . . the* **Boy** *looks closer and finds expensive items of jewellery still in their boxes, looted from the store and discarded.*

The **Boy** *sits, he looks like he's given up, and then:*

Boy   Papa? Papa, we wouldn't ever eat anybody, would we?

Man   No. Of course not.

Boy   No matter how hungry we were? Even if we were starving?

Man   We're starving now.

Boy   Because, because we're the good guys?

Man   Yes.

Boy   And we're carrying the fire.

Man   Yes.

The **Man** *takes the* **Boy** *in his arms. In a moment the* **Boy** *starts blinking sleepily and drifts off to sleep, and the* **Man** *strokes the sleeping* **Boy**'s *hair and kisses him on the forehead.*

The Road

They walk through the parking lot until they come to a supermarket round the other side. A few old cars in a trash-strewn parking lot. The **Man** *heads through the defunct automatic doors.*

Man   Come on. There's nobody here.

INT. SUPERMARKET – DAY

The **Man** *and the* **Boy** *trudge the empty aisles, only litter remaining, the once brightly coloured packaging strewn around, its contents long since looted.*

In the empty gun section there is a deer's head mounted on the wall. The **Boy** *stops and stares, mesmerised, while the* **Man** *searches the empty shelves for ammo, finding only empty boxes.*

The **Man** *glimpses a woman's face staring dolefully from an aisle – an emaciated, dead-beat* **Scavenger** *watching them, vanishing as quickly as she appeared.*

On their way out they come to a pair of vending machines tipped over, the sodas looted, coins scattered around in the ash. The **Man** *sits beside one and feels inside the gutted machine, eventually producing a single unopened can of Coca-Cola.*

Boy (*excited*)   What is it, Papa?

Man   It's a treat for you. Here. Sit down.

He helps the little **Boy** *off with his knapsack and sits him down and opens the can of Coke ceremoniously. The* **Boy** *looks startled and sniffs the fizzing can as if it's the strangest thing he's ever seen in his life.*

Man   Go ahead.

The **Boy** *takes the can.*

Boy   It's bubbly.

Man   Go ahead. Drink it.

The **Boy** *takes a sip and considers.*

Boy   It's really good. You have some, Papa.

Man   No. I want you to drink it.

Boy   But I want you to have some.

The **Man** *reluctantly takes the can and has a tiny sip, hands it back to the wary* **Boy**.

It's because I'll never get to drink another one, isn't it?

The **Man** *doesn't know what to say.*

EXT. MALL/PARKING LOT – LATE AFTERNOON

They head out of the mall now towards the road; lifeless traffic lights at the intersection, town houses and apartment blocks on the other side of the road. The **Boy** *stops to listen, stares around, suddenly energised, bobbing on his toes.*

Man   What's wrong with you?

Boy   What was that?

Man   I didn't hear anything.

Boy   Listen.

Man   I don't hear anything.

They listen more until, very faintly we hear a dog bark in the distance. The **Boy** *turns around 180 degrees to listen, alert with anticipation.*

It's a dog.

Boy (*excited*)   A dog! Where did it come from?

Man   I don't know. Come on.

The **Man** *walks across the road, past the apartments and the* **Boy** *follows, bouncing up and down, over-excited now.*

Boy   We're not going to kill it, are we, Papa?

Man   What? No, we're not going to kill it. Why did you say that?

The Road

Boy   You still got one bullet left.

Man   We're not going to hurt the dog, I promise. We're not going to kill it and we're not going to eat it either.

Boy (*over-excited, not frightened*)   Maybe it'll eat us!

Man   I doubt it very much.

Boy   Can we look for it?

Man   It's gone, okay?

EXT. SUBURBS – DAY

They trudge through the suburbs on the edge of the city, past what used to be the local ball park, now barren, dead, a vast flat expanse of ash and cracked, scorched earth, forlorn stands and bleachers blackened by ash and soot.

Boy   What is it?

Man   I used to watch the ball games here with my father.

EXT. SUBURBAN STREET – DAY

They walk up a once tree-lined suburban street, barren now; ash and dust layer what used to be front lawns, postboxes, picket fences, porches, crazy paving.

*The **Man** stops outside a typical suburban clapboard house with a dead, cracked yard where the lawn used to be and a bare flagpole. The **Boy** eyes the **Man** enquiringly.*

Boy   What is this place, Papa?

Man   It's the house where I grew up.

*They go up to the house – clapboards have been removed for firewood, leaving studs and insulation exposed. The **Boy** stops, reluctant to go further, and the **Man** takes a few more steps, then turns around to check on him.*

You coming?

Boy   I don't want to.

Man   Don't you want to see where I grew up?

Boy   There might be somebody in there.

Man   There's nobody there now.

*The **Man** takes the **Boy**'s hand and they approach a basketball hoop by the garage. The **Man** is momentarily overcome with emotion as he recalls the details, but it doesn't mean much to the* **Boy***.*

*After a moment the **Man** goes up the steps – frightened, but horribly compelled at the same time. The **Boy** follows nervously.*

Boy   I'm scared.

Man   We've got to find something to eat or we'll die.

Boy   I'm not hungry. I'm not!

*The **Man** takes his revolver from his belt and approaches the front door, warily pushing it open.*

Man   Come on.

*He goes through the front door – the **Boy** stays where he is, rigid with fear. The **Boy** notices a stuffed toy dog in the window, staring out at the garden and his curiosity takes over. The **Boy** goes inside carefully.*

INT. DINING ROOM/HOME – DAY

*The pine panelling is stripped from the walls. There is some broken furniture but much has been taken for firewood. They go over to the fireplace and the **Man** examines it. He runs his fingers along the mantel, where there is an old drawing pin still stuck in the wood, nostalgia overcoming his fear.*

Man   This is where we used to have Christmas when I was a boy. We'd hang our stockings right here.

*The **Man** examines the yellow-tiled surround. The **Boy** watches the **Man** as if he's gone mad.*

My mother scrubbed these every day. It's still spotless.

Much of the woodwork and the floorboards have been stripped and taken for firewood – there are gaping holes.

By the fireplace is a small pile of bones – and in the grid are more burnt bones and the skull from the family cat. The **Man** *takes it all in sadly, but the* **Boy** *is unmoved.*

Boy   Papa? I don't think we should do this.

Man   You want to wait outside?

The **Boy** *nods vigorously.*

All right.

He takes the **Boy**'s *hand and leads him out.*

EXT. PORCH/HOME – DAY

The come out on to the porch.

Man   Sit here on the stoop and don't go away.

The **Boy** *sits quietly and the* **Man** *goes back inside. After a moment he starts going through his knapsack, less afraid now.*

INT. OLD HOUSE – DAY

The floorboards creak horribly, swollen from rain or ripped up, as he creeps into the living room. The timber cladding is stripped from the walls, the ceiling plaster collapsed, beams exposed. The **Man** *pads through to the kitchen.*

INT. KITCHEN/OLD HOUSE – DAY

The kitchen is similarly dilapidated, the cupboards stripped bare. On a shelf by the window are dusty jars of fruit, preserved. He grabs a jar, prises open the lid and finds an oily slick of black mucus floating in the top, like rotted mushroom spores.

He sniffs it suspiciously, holds it up to the light. In the light small black fishhook-shaped spores drift from the top of the jar to the bottom. He replaces the lid, appalled.

EXT. PORCH/OLD HOUSE — DAY

*The **Boy** is sitting on the steps of the porch, drawing with crayons on a pad taken from his knapsack. Across the road is another big old house, much of the clapboard missing, swathed in dead brambles. The **Boy** suddenly looks up and stares at it, distracted.*

EXT. BACK YARD — DAY

*The **Man** comes outside and regards the deadened yard, old garden hoe and spade, gardening equipment and a dead apple tree. He goes over and examines the ashen ground and digs about to unearth a couple of small, dark brown, shrivelled spheres spaced several feet apart – apples. He bends down and picks them up, examines, sniffs and stuffs them in his pockets.*

EXT. PORCH/OLD HOUSE — DAY

*The **Boy** is still staring at the house across the road when he notices a ghostly face, completely still, in a window. The **Boy** drops the pad and crayon and stands, surprised, not believing his eyes – it is the face of a **Small Boy** roughly his age, which disappears almost immediately, receding back into the gloom like a ghost.*

INT. PANTRY/CLAPBOARD HOUSE — DAY

*The **Man** is in the looted pantry. He finds some shrivelled raisins that have spilt, hidden in the back of the shelf. He puts them into a handkerchief, folds it and pockets it. He hears:*

Boy (*out of vision*)   Stop – stop!

*The **Man** freezes, then charges out.*

The Road

*The **Man** rushes out and stares about frantically for the **Boy**. He's gone.*

EXT. HOUSE OPPOSITE – DAY

*The **Boy** has run across the road to another house.*

***Boy**'s point of view – peeping around the side of the house is the other **Small Boy**, the same age, similarly grimy and thin, wearing an outsize woollen coat. The other **Small Boy** disappears down the side and the **Boy** runs after him.*

Boy   Wait! Come back! I won't hurt you!

EXT. BACK YARD – DAY

*The **Boy** runs to the bottom of the yard where there is various suburban garden detritus: a dusty lawnmower, a clothes line, a shed, bikes with no tyres.*

Boy   Where are you?!

*The **Man** comes sprinting up the side of the house and seizes him by the arm.*

Man   What are you doing? What the hell are you doing?

Boy   There's a little boy, Papa, I saw a little boy.

Man   There's no little boy. What's the matter with you?

Boy   Yes there is! I saw him! A boy just like me.

*The **Man** takes the **Boy** by the arm and drags him back through the yard, up the side of the house, the **Boy** resisting, crying and looking back all the way.*

Boy   Why? Why can't I go and see him?

EXT. HOUSE – DAY

Out the front of the house the **Boy** *digs his heels in and the* **Man** *has to drag him, his feet slithering through the dirt.*

Boy   I need to see him! I need to!

Man   Why?

Boy   I just do!

The **Boy** *has gone limp, weeping bitterly, resisting being moved. The* **Man** *gives up and squats beside the sobbing* **Boy**.

Man   Okay, I'm sorry. I understand.

He holds him, wipes his tears from his cheeks.

EXT. TOWN STREET/OVERPASS – EVENING

In the failing light they come across a late model Chevy, abandoned under an overpass.

Boy   Papa? Will there be other boys like me at the coast?

Man   I hope so.

The **Man** *goes to the car, wipes thick dust from the windscreen and peers in – it's empty.*

INT. CHEVY – NIGHT

They try to get comfortable in the leather seats, the **Man** *spreading the blankets over them and tucking the* **Boy** *in.*

They are quiet a moment as they watch darkness start to fall. Then:

Man   I got you something

The **Man** *produces from his pocket one of the tiny hard brown apples and holds it up to the remaining light.*

Boy   What is it?

The Road

Man It's an apple.

He hands it to the boy who examines it curiously. The **Man**
*takes out a pocket knife, takes the apple back, cuts the apple in
half to reveal a woody brown interior. They regard the mahogany
apple uncertainly; the* **Man** *is the first to take a bite, with some
difficulty. The* **Boy** *bites his half and makes a face.*

Man Suck it a while and it'll soften.

They sit sucking and chewing the ancient apple.

Boy Did you ever have any friends?

The **Man** *eyes the* **Boy** *– curious at the sudden question.*

Man Yes. I did.

Boy Lots of them?

Man Yes . . .

Boy Do you remember them?

Man Yes. I remember all of them . . .

Boy What happened to them?

Man They died.

Boy All of them?

Man Yes. All of them.

EXT. URBAN ENVIRONS (MONTAGE) – DAY

The **Man** *and the* **Boy** *make their way out of the outskirts of
the ruined city.*

Man (*voice-over*) He yearns for his own friends and
imagines how things will be different at the coast – and
that there will be other children there . . . When I have
nothing else, I try to dream the dreams of a child's
imaginings . . .

EXT. DESOLATE ROAD — DAY

*The **Man** and the **Boy** walk along a desolate road in what was once farmland. Grain silos loom ominously, still standing.*

Boy   Do you know where we are, Papa?

Man   I think we're about two hundred miles from the coast. As the crow flies.

Boy   'As the crow flies'?

Man   It means, going in a straight line.

Man's *point of view — in the background, something catches his eye and he focuses on:*

A frieze of human heads, dried with taut grins and shrunken eyes, perched on wooden poles. Some are tattooed with targets and runic slogans. Some are skinless, with signs and words inked on to them. One has suture marks etched on it, like a blueprint for assembly.

Boy   There aren't any crows are there? Just in books.

Man   Yeah, just in books . . .

*The **Man** stares at the heads as the **Boy** continues his conversation, distracted and not seeing the heads.*

Boy   Do you think there might be crows somewhere?

Man   I don't know . . .

Boy   But what do you think?

Man   I think it's unlikely . . .

*They keep walking and talking, the **Man** grim-faced but the **Boy** intent on what's ahead.*

Boy   Could they fly to Mars or some place?

Man   No, they couldn't fly to Mars.

Boy   Because it's too far?

Man   Yes.

The Road

*The **Man** discreetly hurries the **Boy** on with a guiding hand towards the woods and off the road.*

Boy   What if they tried and – and – and they just got halfway or something and then they were too tired? Would they fall back down . . . ?

EXT. EDGE OF WOODS – EVENING

*On the edge of the wood the **Man** and the **Boy** stop to examine footprints in the snow.*

*The **Man** listens and hears: the low thudding of bull drums in the distance. He looks at the exhausted **Boy** a moment.*

Man   We can't go back on the road.

Boy   Why, Papa?

Man   I think someone's coming.

*The **Boy** stares at the tracks. The **Man** stares in both directions, examining the road in the distance. He moves a few paces and notices, tied to a dead sapling, a thin red neckerchief. He takes a few steps and through a gap in the trees sees a clearing – snow and a mass of blood-red footprints, the icy snow stained blood-red like a sorbet. A killing floor.*

Boy   Will they see our tracks?

Man   We'll cover them.

*The **Man** moves the **Boy** away and kicks snow over their tracks, then lays fresh ones going in several different directions. The **Boy** copies him, leaving his own maze of tracks. They run off, keeping parallel with the road but staying off it.*

Man's *point of view – in the distance two **Figures** appear on the road.*

Here they come.

*The **Man** now looks over his shoulder for a good look, then grabs the **Boy**'s hand and takes off.*

EXT. HIGH GROUND — EVENING

*Two **Men** come prowling on the road: they are **Militants** from some sort of army, wearing the same red neckerchiefs and carrying weapons, searching, predatory.*

*Wider — we see that only thirty feet away, concealed among the trees, the **Man** and **Boy** are crouched in blankets, watching. The two **Militants** stop and look around, as if they sense the **Boy** and the **Man** — who freeze, frightened to breathe. The **Militants** sniff the air menacingly.*

*One of them walks over to a stone by the side of the road, leans down and starts sharpening his lance, made from the straightened coil-spring of a car. The **Man** and the **Boy** watch, wide-eyed. Eventually the **Militants** walk off up the road.*

Boy   What are we going to do?

No answer.

EXT. DEEP IN THE WOODS — EVENING

*There is a thick carpet of grey snow. The **Man** lays out a tarp on the ground and blankets on top. Out of the murky sky more grey snow is falling. The **Man** is distracted by a sudden noise, the loud crack of shearing wood — this time very close. He looks around just as:*

Out of nowhere a tree branch sails down, barely missing them, landing with a heavy whump just feet away.

Man   Move! Quickly!

*He tries to get the **Boy** to his feet, but he is limp, staring around blearily, exhausted.*

*They hear another loud whump. Then the groan of timber and another whump as trees start to keel over around them. The **Man** grabs the **Boy** and runs as best he can through the snow and falling trees. They have abandoned their blankets, tarp and backpacks.*

Boy   What's happening?

Man   Just keep moving, run!

*They rush through the woods as more and more trees fall one after the other, whump, whump, whump, great loads of snow falling from limbs to the ground with a boom, setting the woods shuddering. The **Boy** is getting bogged in the snow and the **Man** stoops and scoops up the **Boy**, and they cram themselves under a fat fallen tree to shield themselves.*

EXT. SEWER PIPE/EMBANKMENT, SNOWDRIFT – NIGHT

They are huddled inside a huge sewer pipe, sheltering.

*The **Boy** is wrapped up inside the **Man**'s coat, wet and shivering, wide awake, nerves shredded, too anxious to lie down and sleep now.*

*The **Man** boils water in a car hubcap.*

He takes from his pocket the handkerchief filled with raisins, offers them.

Boy   That's all there is, isn't it?

Man   Yes.

Boy   There's nothing left anywhere.

Man   No.

They sit eating raisins, saying nothing until they've finished.

Boy   Can I ask you something?

Man   Sure.

Boy   Are we going to die now?

*The **Man** just looks at the **Boy**, then looks away.*

Man   What do you think is going to happen? We're just going to suddenly keel over and die? It takes a long time to die of starvation. The important thing is water to stop you dehydrating. We've got water. We'll be all right.

EXT. OUTSKIRTS OF TOWN – MORNING

Snowed-in farmland, in the background a row of fallen and crumpled high-tension electrical towers. A town in the far distance ahead of the **Boy** *and the* **Man**. *The* **Boy** *is hunched over with a hunger cramp. They are both wet and shivering. The* **Man** *eyes the* **Boy** *anxiously.*

EXT. PATIO / TOWN HOUSE – DAY

The **Man** *stands on the back patio of a house on the edge of town, the* **Boy** *at his side, fields stretching out before them, the land flattened and dead, ravaged fences running the perimeter. In the yard are a few dead trees, a fence, a metal toolshed, an old barbecue on the patio made from a forty-four-gallon drum. The* **Man** *slides the patio door open and peers inside gingerly.*

INT. BEDROOM / TOWN HOUSE – DAY

The **Man** *is in the bedroom looking around for useful things. It has been stripped, the wooden frame gone from the window, the bureau ransacked and chopped up – only a summer dress on a wire hanger on the back of the door remains. He glances at empty drawers on the floor and a cupboard before turning his attention to the bed.*

He blinks and sways a moment, trying to focus on:

Man*'s point of view – underneath the filthy, dusty blankets a thin, dried head pokes out, the blankets pulled up to the chin. On the pillow are long hunks of rotted hair. Next to the bed are rotting and empty travel bags.*

Man (*voice-over*)   Every day is a lie. But I am slowly dying. That is not a lie . . . I am trying to prepare him for the day when I am gone.

He takes hold of the lower hem of the blanket and throws it off the bed, revealing a desiccated corpse. He ignores it, shaking the blanket out and folding it under his arm. He notices the boy at his side, watching wide-eyed.

The Road

Man   Nothing you haven't seen before.

They go out.

INT. KITCHEN/TOWN HOUSE – DAY

*The **Man** opens and shuts empty cupboards, slamming the
doors, increasingly desperate, close to tears of frustration now.
Eventually he feels dizzy and has to sit on the floor. He just sits
there, alone on the kitchen floor, clenching and unclenching his
fists, his head in his hands, when he hears:*

Boy (*out of vision*)   Papa!

*The **Man** draws his pistol and goes out, alert again.*

INT. TOWN HOUSE – DAY

*The **Boy** is staring at himself in a dusty, flyblown full-length
mirror. As the **Man** comes in he sees the **Boy**'s reflection and his
own and jumps.*

Boy   It's us.

*The **Boy** stares at his reflection – he looks like an alien, skinny
with giant staring eyes on shaky legs.*

We look skinny.

Man   We are skinny.

*The **Man** puts the blanket around the **Boy**'s shoulders. He
notices an old upright piano, covered in ash and dust. The **Boy**
stares as he goes to it, lifts the lid and plays a chord.*

*The **Boy**'s eyes light up and he is magnetised, instantly coming
over and waiting for the next note. The **Man** plays another
chord.*

Boy   What is it?

Man   It's a piano.

Boy   What's it for?

Man   For making music. This . . . (*He plays.*) is music. Your mother played very well.

Boy   I don't remember.

Man   Before you were born. We had one just like it. It was beautiful.

Boy   What happened to it?

Man   Chopped it up for firewood.

He stares into space, slumps suddenly, overcome with emotion as he remembers.

INT. CLAPBOARD HOUSE – DAY

*Flashback – the **Man** and the pregnant **Woman** alone in the house, just before the **Boy** was born. Some of the furniture has been broken up for firewood – there are broken pieces by the fire and a huge axe propped on the hearth. The **Woman** stands at the piano and tries to play. She plays for a moment and the **Man** cracks a rare smile – the piano is out of tune and she stops. She plays a bit more but soon starts to bang the keys atonally in frustration. The **Man** just lets her get on with it until she's spent.*

Woman   I used to worry what would happen if there was a fire. What would I save? What could I bear to lose? There used to be so many things, so many beautiful things. Things people made. Things nature made. Who knew we would lose it all?

Man   I'll strip the floorboards.

Woman   You can't live without a floor.

Man   You can't live without a piano.

She starts to dismantle the piano, opening the lid, taking it off its hinges; it's heavy. She hands him the heavy lid and he reluctantly dumps it on the floor.

Woman   It's my piano.

Man I bought it for you.

Woman It needs tuning. Who's going to tune it? Can you tune it?

They look at each other sadly. They take the front piece away and dump that. The **Woman** *picks up the axe and hands it to the* **Man**. *He swings it at the frame.*

End of flashback.

EXT. YARD — DAY

The **Man** *walks towards a tin shed and crosses the dead grass. He stops suddenly. He stamps about a bit, listening. He continues on into the shed. Beside the shed sits an industrial garden trolley. The man reappears, spade in hand. He digs the spade into the dead grass and hears it chomp into wood. He digs more urgently, increasingly exhausted, until a door is revealed in the dirt. He is so engrossed he hasn't noticed the* **Boy** *standing a few feet away, watching with saucer eyes, scared.*

Boy Don't open it, Papa.

Man It'll be okay.

Boy Please, Papa, please.

Man It's okay.

Boy No it's not! What if there's people hiding down there?

The **Man** *ignores him, focused as he chops the plywood around the lock, gets the spade under a corner and levers the door open. The* **Boy** *has his fists bunched up to his chest, bobbing up and down with fear.*

The **Man** *starts to descend a hand-made wooden staircase in the bunker. He takes another disposable lighter from his pocket, gives the child a kiss on the forehead and then disappears into the bunker, leaving the worried* **Boy** *staring after him. The* **Boy** *looks around at the deserted yard as the evening draws in, now even more frightened.*

Man (*out of vision*)   Oh my God . . . Oh my God!

Boy   What is it, Papa?

Man (*out of vision*)   Come down. Oh my God, come down.

*The **Boy** is in the hole and down the steps like lightning.*

INT. BUNKER — EVENING

*The little **Boy** clatters down the steps. The **Man** is busy lighting up candles.*

Boy   Papa? What did you find?

Man   Everything. I found everything.

Stored in the bunker are crate upon crate of canned goods: tomatoes, peaches, beans, apricots, canned ham, corned beef, hundreds of gallons of water in jerry cans; and, in boxes, paper towels, toilet paper and trash bags stuffed with blankets.

*The **Man** takes the **Boy**'s hand and helps him down, then goes back up the steps and draws the door shut and jams a pair of metal pliers through the heavy inside hasp to stop the door being opened. He goes back down the steps to the **Boy** and holds up a candle to illuminate the shelves.*

Man   Can you see?

Boy   What is all this stuff?

Man   It's food! Can you read the labels?

*The **Boy** stares at the brightly coloured packaging; he's never seen anything like it before. The **Man** hands the **Boy** a tin.*

Boy   'Pears'. It says 'Pears'.

Man   Yes! It does! Oh yes it does! Pears!

*They inspect the shelves: chilli, corn, stew, soup, spaghetti sauce. The **Boy**'s eyes are like saucers.*

Boy   Is it real?

Man   Oh yes, it's real all right.

The Road

*The **Man** pulls a box of butane lighters from the shelf and tests one; it doesn't work. He tests another which works; it has a large flame – he uses it to read the labels.*

Boy   Why is it here?

Man   Because someone thought it might be needed.

Boy   But they died.

Man   Yes. What would you like for breakfast?

Boy (*thinks*)   Pears.

Man   Pears it is.

*The **Man** claws open a box and pulls out a tin of pears. He gets paper bowls from a stack, plastic forks and spoons, lays them out. He finds a camping lamp.*

*He puts a butane canister in and lights up the lamp. He finds a can-opener and opens the pears while the **Boy** watches silently, wrapping a blanket around himself and sitting on the soft bunk bed.*

Boy   Is it okay for us to take it?

Man   They'd want us to.

*The **Man** dishes up two bowls of pears and they sit side by side on the bunk with spoons and pears.*

These will be the best pears you ever tasted. The best. You just wait.

*They eat in silence. They lick the spoons and drink the syrup from the bowls. The **Man** feels inside his mouth with his fingers – the sugar irritating a sore tooth.*

Too sweet.

*The **Boy** smiles, amused, and the **Man** opens another tin.*

INT. BUNKER – EVENING

*Ham and powdered eggs frying in a pan on the camping stove. The kettle is boiling on another ring of the gas stove. The **Boy** just stares at the bubbling food as the **Man** cooks.*

Nearby a breakfast table is set out on a stack of boxes acting as a breakfast bar: biscuits, a plate of margarine, condensed milk, salt and pepper, plates and utensils. The **Man** *brings the pan over and forks over chunks of ham on to the plates, then spoonfuls of scrambled eggs from a second pan, then baked beans from a small pot. The* **Boy** *just stares, as if drugged, uncomprehending, the food alien to him.*

Man Go ahead. Don't let it get cold.

Boy What do I eat first?

Man Whatever you like.

The **Boy** *eats a hunk of ham as the* **Man** *pours coffee.*

Boy Is this coffee?

Man That's right. Careful, it's hot.

He hands him coffee.

Boy We did good, didn't we, Papa?

Man Yeah, we did good.

INT. BUNKER – NIGHT

The **Man** *puts the* **Boy** *to bed in a bunk and smooths his filthy hair tenderly, smiling with relief, until the* **Boy** *shuts his eyes and nods off. He covers the* **Boy** *with a blanket and kisses him. He just sits watching the* **Boy** *sleep, suddenly on the verge of tears.*

INT. BUNKER – NIGHT

The **Man** *folds the* **Boy**'s *tiny clothes, noticing the bulging pockets of his pants. He empties them, creating a small pile of collected artefacts: a smooth stone, a marble, an old house key, bottle tops, a smooth, hand-made Indian arrowhead, fashioned from stone, lastly a broken piece of a woman's mother-of-pearl hair comb.*

By the **Boy**'s *bunk he unfolds the crayon drawing he's been working on and examines it, deeply moved.*

The Road

Man's point of view – an eccentric, childlike drawing of the **Woman**, skinny like a stick figure but, inexplicably, with a brightly smiling face and big laughing eyes, labelled simply 'Mom' in spidery scrawl.

Stirring classical music fades up and into:

INT. THEATRE – EVENING

Flashback – close in on a pair of legs in stockings, a summer dress, a **Woman**'s hands holding a **Man**'s hand in her lap. The **Man** feels the tops of the stockings with his fingers.

Wider – the **Man** is with the **Woman** in a concert theatre, at a recital. The **Woman** wears the mother-of-pearl hair comb. The seats are velvet, gold scrollwork adorns the boxes, an illustrious, fortunate world.

End of flashback.

INT. BUNKER – MORNING

The **Boy** wakes blearily and immediately notices his collection of artefacts turfed out by the bed.

Nearby the **Man** is dressing as the **Boy** starts gathering up his collection crossly, especially protective of the arrowhead, or just embarrassed. They look at each other.

Man   What?

Boy   Don't touch my stuff.

EXT. LAWN – MORNING

The hatch opens and the **Man**'s face appears as he looks around. He opens the hatch further and clambers out with a couple of jerry cans of water. The yard is quiet. Next, the **Boy**'s face pops up and peers around. He clambers out carrying a big pot with a camping stove in it.

INT. BATHROOM, TOWN HOUSE — MORNING

They empty the jerry cans into the huge pot, light the stove and put the pot on the stove to heat the water.

INT. BATHROOM, TOWN HOUSE — MORNING

*The **Boy** is in the bath, filthy and scrawny, as the **Man** bathes him, rubbing him with soap, scrubbing an oily film of scum from his dirty neck to reveal clean pale skin underneath.*

Man   What do you think?

Boy   Nice and warm.

*He washes the **Boy**'s hair, lathering water over him with the pot. He has a sudden thought.*

Cut to:

INT. BATHROOM/CLAPBOARD HOUSE — DAY

*Flashback – the **Man** watches unseen from the doorway as the **Woman** tenderly washes the **Boy**'s hair – he is perhaps a year younger than at the start of the film. She appears lost in the task, enjoying it, chatting away to the **Boy**, momentarily unburdened. She sticks a finger in the **Boy**'s ears, giving them a good soaping, which he likes.*

Woman   You could grow potatoes in these ears . . .

INT. BATHROOM, TOWN HOUSE — DAY

*End flashback – now the **Man** is in the tub, also scrawny and filthy, lost in thought as he soaps up. The **Boy** helps.*

INT. BATHROOM, TOWN HOUSE — DAY

*The **Man** trims his beard off with scissors in a mirror. He lathers up with shaving cream and starts to shave with a plastic*

safety razor. When the **Man** *is done he turns to the* **Boy**,
wiping away the foam.

Man   How do I look?

Boy   Weird. Won't you be cold?

INT. BATHROOM, TOWN HOUSE – DAY

Now the **Man** *is cutting the* **Boy**'s *hair with kitchen scissors
and a plastic comb. The* **Boy** *has a towel around his shoulders
and long locks of hair decorate it. The* **Man** *finishes, takes the
towel off, wipes the* **Boy**'s *neck and face with a flannel, holds
up a mirror for the* **Boy** *to see.*

Boy   I look funny.

INT. BUNKER – MORNING

*They sit on the bunk bed with a checkerboard between them
sipping thick hot chocolate made with condensed milk from
plastic mugs and concentrating on the board, their worn-out,
wet blue jeans drying on a drying rack in the background.*

*They are both wearing new sweaters too big for them, plundered
from the stores. The* **Man** *watches the* **Boy** *fondly, absorbed in
checkers.*

EXT. LAWN – NIGHT

*Heavy rain slashes down on the lawn. Already pools of water
are flooding the lawn.*

INT. BUNKER – NIGHT

*A shiny new quart of whisky is slipped from its paper liquor
store bag and opened with a soft crack. The whisky is poured
into a glass with a satisfying glug.*

*Wider – another feast is laid out, ham and powdered mashed
potato and biscuits and gravy. The* **Boy** *is eating while the*

Man *pours a whisky. The* **Boy** *stops eating to watch the* **Man** *drink the whisky. The* **Man***'s eyes glaze as he sips the strong liquor, dizzy already.*

Boy Can I try some?

Man No. You won't like it. Makes you feel funny.

The **Boy** *stares, curious, wanting it.*

You think I come from another world, don't you?

Filled with all these strange things you've never seen.

Boy Sort of.

Man Well, I do I guess.

EXT. LAWN — EVENING

The **Man** *just stands in the middle of the lawn, coughing his guts up in the dark rain – again the phlegmy wet cough. He bends over, sweating, listening, knowing it's the sound of fluid on the lungs.*

As he listens he hears something above the rain. He keeps shifting position, as if hearing different sounds from different directions. Nevertheless he anxiously looks around, then goes to the porch and drags an old mattress over, across the dead grass to the hatch.

He lays it half-across the hatch, crawls through the remaining gap and hauls the mattress the rest of the way over the hatch, then pulls the hatch closed with the old mattress lying on top. It just looks like an old mattress lying on a lawn in the rain.

INT. BUNKER — DAWN

The **Man** *listens to the patter of rain and hears another sound: something or someone rustling around the mattress above. He hears the sound of the mattress being dragged off the door. He hears scrabbling and scratching on the door and freezes, staring at the lock, waiting for the inevitable . . . He quietly picks up the revolver. He looks across and sees the* **Boy** *is now wide awake too, staring, wide-eyed.*

Boy What is it?

Man Shh.

Boy (*whispers*) Maybe it's a dog.

Man (*whispers*) It's not a dog.

Boy (*barely managing to whisper*) It is! It's a dog! A dog!

*The **Man** listens anxiously as the pawing and scratching continues, the wood over the bunker amplifying the noise. He cocks the revolver and positions himself under the hatch, ready.*

Man If it's a dog it'll be with someone.

Boy Who?

Man I don't know.

After a tortuous moment the sounds die away.

Man I'm not waiting to find out. Come on. Let's get out of here.

Boy I don't want to go.

Man I know, but it's not safe any more.

*The **Man** grabs his gun and cocks it, rushes about turning out all the lamps, and they sit anxiously in the darkness.*

EXT. LAWN – MORNING

*Later – it's now lighter outside, the mattress lifts as the **Man** opens the trap door and very carefully peeps out. He looks around, all angles, checking the coast is clear, then shuts the hatch again.*

INT. BUNKER – MORNING

*The **Man** starts loading cans and packets into a carton. He gathers a couple of large jerry cans of water. The **Boy** helps.*

Boy What are we going to do with all this stuff?

Man We'll just have to take what we can.

Boy I wish we could live here. And we could keep the dog and the dog could catch food for us.

Man Look, there is no dog, okay? I'm sorry, but there just isn't.

Boy Well what is it!

Man I don't know what it is!

Boy Please, Papa.

Man No.

Boy Just say it's going to be all right, Papa. Say it. Just say it, please.

The **Man** *doesn't know what to say, losing patience.*

Man Listen, trouble comes when you least expect it. So maybe the thing to do is to just always expect it.

Boy Do you always expect it? Papa?

Man I do, yes.

Boy You always think bad things are going to happen, but we found this place. Maybe we'll find another place like this at the coast.

Man Maybe.

The **Man** *dumps the carton of food on the floor and packs another, organising jerry cans of water.*

EXT. LAWN – MORNING

The industrial trolley is loaded up and tied with a grey tarp, a tyre pump leaning against it.

Boy What are you doing?

Man We'll have to cover our tracks from now on.

The **Man** *drags the old mattress back over the entrance to the bunker. He carefully covers the surrounding area with debris.*

The Road

*The **Man** pulls the new trolley across a bridge, stagnant black water underneath. The trolley is now laden with jerry cans of fresh water and cartons containing as many tins of food and supplies as they could manage. The **Boy** trails along behind.*

*They are a strange sight, clean-clothed, clean-shaven, short-haired, in their new jumpers – and now both wearing new surgical masks which they raise off their faces to speak. The **Man** keeps checking behind him.*

***Man**'s point of view – he sees the glint of glass, perhaps a pair of binoculars watching them.*

*The **Boy** watches anxiously as the **Man** gets out his own binoculars and looks through them.*

***Man**'s point of view – a mysterious winking glint of light which quickly disappears.*

*Through a different pair of binoculars, a completely different point of view: we see the **Man** looking through his binoculars at us.*

Man   I think they're following us.

Boy   Who?

Man   I don't know.

Boy   You think it's bad guys?

Man   Probably.

Boy   What if it's good guys?

Man   I don't think we're likely to meet any good guys for a while. We have to be careful now. We've got food.

EXT. BEND/THE ROAD – DAY

*As they round a bend in the road they see a hunched **Figure** walking ahead of them. The **Man** stops abruptly, gets out the binoculars and watches.*

***Man**'s point of view – a distant, hunched **Figure** hobbling away from them.*

EXT. ROAD – DAY

They come up behind an **Old Man**, *hunched over, withered, silent, as he hobbles ahead. He wears layers of torn clothing and his feet are wrapped in rags and cardboard tied with green twine. They slowly approach and the* **Old Man** *stops, turns and watches them suspiciously as they draw level.*

Old Man   I don't have anything for you. You can look if you want. I got nothing.

Man   We're not robbers.

The **Old Man** *leans an ear forward, deaf.*

Old Man   What?

Man   I said we're not robbers.

Old Man   What are you?

Man   We're just like you.

Old Man   What are you following me for?

Man   We're not following you.

Boy   We've got food we could give him.

Man   He's not getting any food.

The **Old Man** *looks away, avoiding their eyes.*

Boy   He's scared, Papa.

Man   Everybody's scared.

Boy   Please, Papa.

Man   All right!

The **Man** *eyes the road to the left and right, then draws his revolver.*

If this is an ambush, he goes first.

He goes out to the trolley and rummages in it while the **Boy** *and the* **Old Man** *stare at each other.*

The **Man** *comes back with a tin of fruit cocktail and a can-opener and opens it and hands it to the* **Boy**. *The* **Boy** *places the tin of fruit on the road in front of the* **Old Man**.

The Road

Boy Take it. Here.

*The **Old Man** doesn't move.*

What about a spoon?

Man He's not getting a spoon.

*The **Boy** urges him on, miming with his hands, as if feeding a raccoon.*

Boy Eat it. It's good.

*The **Old Man** picks up the tin and his filthy long nails clatter on the tin as he tips it to his mouth, the juice running down his chin, his head jerking as he swallows.*

Boy Look, Papa. He's hungry.

Man I see it. And I know what you're going to ask me. And the answer is no.

Boy What's the question?

Man We can't keep him.

*They watch him eating painfully slowly. The **Old Man** finishes and sits down in the road holding the tin, staring at it, as if it might refill.*

Man When did you last eat?

*The **Old Man** just stares.*

Man Do you want to eat with us?

Old Man I don't know. What do I have to do?

Man Tell us where the world went.

Old Man What?

Man You don't have to do anything. Can you walk okay?

*They help the **Old Man** off the road and hand him his cane but he pushes it away.*

Old Man I can walk.

They walk off the road towards the dead, blackened woods.

EXT. WOODS – DAY

As they leave the road the **Old Man** *studies the* **Boy**. *The* **Boy** *goes to take his hand.*

Man (*to* **Boy**) Don't hold his hand.

Boy He can't see.

Man Don't.

The trio walk into the woods.

How old are you?

Old Man I'm ninety.

Man Ninety my ass. Is that what you tell people? So they don't hurt you?

Old Man Uh-huh.

Man Does it work?

Old Man Nope.

Man What's your name?

Old Man Ely.

Man Just 'Ely'?

Old Man What's wrong with 'Ely'?

EXT. CLEARING/WOODS – EVENING

There's a camp fire now. The **Old Man** *sits wrapped in a quilt, eating with a spoon and licking his plate clean. In the far distance, the faint glow of fires. The orange light bounces into the night sky eerily.*

Man How come you're still alive? What do you eat?

Old Man I don't know. People give you things.

Man No they don't.

Old Man You did.

Man   I didn't. He did.

The **Old Man** *eyes the* **Boy**, *closely, half blind.*

Old Man   Are you a little boy?

Man   What does he look like?

Old Man   I don't know. I can't see real good.

Man   Is that right? Can you see me?

Old Man   No. But I can tell somebody's there.

Man (*to* **Boy**)   Okay. You need to sleep. Come on.

He gathers up the **Boy** *and takes him a few feet away, settles him down in blankets while the* **Old Man** *stares into the fire. When the* **Man** *returns he has his gun, which he surreptitiously places on the ground in full view of the* **Old Man**.

Man   You can see that, right? Okay. Tell me now. You're not a shill for a pack of road agents?

Old Man   I'm not anything. I'll go if you want me to. I can find the road.

The **Man** *stares at the* **Old Man** *cynically, but the* **Old Man** *just stares back blankly.*

I live like an animal. You don't want to know the things I've had to eat. When I saw that boy I thought I'd died and he was an angel. I never thought I'd see a child again. I never thought that would happen to me.

Man   He is an angel. To me he's a god.

Old Man   Well, I hope that's not true. To be on the road with the last surviving god would be a pretty frightening experience.

Man   Why do you say that?

Old Man   Where men can't live, gods can't either. The road gangs would tear you limb from limb, both of you.

The low rumble in the earth is heard again, an earthquake, this time in the distance. They listen a moment.

I knew this was coming. This or something like it. There were warnings. People thought it was a con – I always believed in it.

Man   Did you try to get ready for it?

Old Man   No. What would you do? Even if you knew what to do, you wouldn't know what to do. Suppose you were the last man left alive?

Man   How would you know if you were the last man alive?

Old Man   I don't guess you would know it. You'd just be it.

Man   Maybe God would know.

Old Man   If there is a God up there he would have turned his back on us by now. Whoever made humanity will find no humanity here.

The **Man** *pours hot water into mugs to make coffee, hands one to the* **Old Man**. *They drink.*

Man   Do you ever wish you would die?

Old Man   No. It's foolish to ask for luxuries in times like these.

Man   Don't you want to end it all?

Old Man   Nope.

Man   Why not?

Old Man   I'm stubborn.

EXT. EDGE OF WOODS – MORNING

The **Boy** *and the* **Old Man** *are standing by the trolley. The* **Man** *is watching from further away. The* **Old Man** *is fitting another can of peaches the* **Boy** *has given him into his knapsack.*

The Road

Man You should thank him, you know. I wouldn't have given you anything.

Old Man Maybe I should and maybe I shouldn't. I wouldn't have given you anything.

*The **Old Man** looks around, orientating himself, and goes, tapping his cane, without a glance back at the **Boy** or the **Man**. The **Man** gives the **Boy** a reproachful look and the **Boy** looks defiant for the first time, a new distance between them.*

Boy He's going to die and you don't care.

Man I care enough. Maybe when we're out of food you'll have more time to think about it.

Boy You always say watch out for bad guys, but that old man wasn't a bad guy and you can't even tell any more.

INT. CHURCH – DAWN

*The **Man** and the **Boy** are camped inside an old church; dusty, faded stained-glass is the only colour, startling after all the monochrome. The **Man** and **Boy** are wrapped up in blankets, a small fire going. The **Boy** is asleep but the **Man** is awake, coughing. He sits up, still coughing. He gets up and walks outside, trying to stifle the coughing.*

INT. CHURCH – DAWN

*The **Man** wanders into an antechamber, coughing uncontrollably, falls to his knees in a shroud of morning mist flooding the church – and coughs up a gob of something dark and nasty, spits it into the misty ground.*

***Man**'s point of view – the mist before him clears to reveal a spattering of dark blood on the pale ash. He stares, shocked, knowing what it signifies.*

74

INT. CHURCH – DAWN

The **Boy** *opens his eyes – he hasn't been asleep, listening to the* **Man** *cough, worried. The* **Man** *returns and eyes the worried* **Boy**.

Man   What's wrong?

Boy   I had a bad dream.

Man   What about?

Boy   I don't want to tell you. Just you.

Man   What happened to me?

The **Boy***'s face crinkles up, he starts to sob.*

The **Man** *coughs again and the* **Boy** *shoots out a hand, puts it over the* **Man***'s mouth to staunch the coughing.*

Man (*voice-over*)   I tell him: When you dream about bad things happening it shows you're still fighting. You're still alive. It's when you start to dream about good things you should start to worry.

EXT. ROAD/RAILWAY LINE, BLACKENED LANDSCAPE – DAY

They are trudging along the blacktop adjacent to a railway line. There is a shotgun blast in the distance and the **Man** *and the* **Boy** *stop and look around. The* **Man** *checks behind him instinctively.*

Man*'s point of view – a thin spike of smoke from a campfire rising up in the woods behind. The* **Boy** *notices and looks behind.*

Boy   Do you think they're still following us?

Man   I think they've been following us for a long time.

Boy   Maybe it's Ely – the old man?

Man   How? On a broomstick?

The **Boy** *thinks about this for a moment as they approach the railway line. The* **Man** *takes the revolver from the trolley and sticks it in his belt – the* **Boy** *notices anxiously.*

We should lay in wait a while. See who they are.

The Road

EXT. RAILWAY BRIDGE, BLACKENED LANDSCAPE — EVENING

*The **Man** and the **Boy** are swaddled in blankets up among the rocks with a bird's eye view of the road and a railway bridge; they can see along the road and the dead trees for half a mile. The **Boy** is nodding off, his head lolling as the **Man** keeps watch, increasingly paranoid.*

EXT. BLUFFS, BLACKENED LANDSCAPE — MORNING

*As they come down from the bluffs, the **Man** is staring into the dead woods where another thin stem of smoke is rising.*

Boy   What is it?

Man   More smoke. I think we should take a look.

Boy   I don't want to. Let's just keep going.

Man   Whoever it is, I don't want them behind us.

Boy   What if they're bad guys?

Man   What if they're good guys?

*They look at each other, a stalemate. The **Man** stands and starts to pack up the tarp.*

Look. Whoever it is out there, it's better to know about it than to not know.

Boy   Why?

Man   Because we don't like surprises. Surprises are scary. They could sneak up on us further down the road. You need to learn this.

*The **Man** folds the tarp and sleeping blankets and starts heading down the slope to the trolley, the **Boy** following.*

EXT. CLEARING, BLACKENED LANDSCAPE — MORNING

*A deserted campsite, a campfire, recently abandoned. The **Man** and the **Boy** look around, disappointed.*

EXT. DUNES/COAST ROAD, BLACKENED LANDSCAPE – DAY

Open country now, completely blackened landscape under heavy ash. They have stopped. The **Boy** *unfolds the threadbare map on the ground, a crayon in his hand.*

Man   You know where we are?

Boy   No.

Man   Where do you think?

The **Boy** *points to a place on the map.*

Man   More.

Boy   Here?

Man   No. We're closer than you think.

He takes the crayon and points on the map.

Man   This is us. This is all sea.

Boy   Is it blue?

Man   The sea? I don't know. It used to be.

The **Man** *picks up a desiccated pine cone from the ground, and stares at it, hollow-eyed, hungry. He squeezes it and it crumbles to dust. He takes a few steps, sniffing the air.*

Can you smell that?

Boy   It smells different.

Man   Everything is going to be different.

EXT. DUNES – DAY

The landscape has changed, dead salt bush and sand at the side of the road and finally, as they come around a bend in the road, dead sea grass sloping up to sand dunes up ahead. They look at each other and head for the dunes excitedly. The **Man** *hides the trolley discreetly, so the* **Boy** *doesn't see his concern. He takes their bags, tarps and blankets with them as they head off for the dunes.*

The Road

EXT. TOP OF SAND DUNE – DAY

Boy's *point of view – grey beach, lead-grey sea and waves rolling in slowly with a distant roar. On the beach a tidemark of wet grey ashy sludge and a skirt of glistening bones, fish skeletons bleached white on the sand.*

They take their parka hoods down and just stand there staring at the beach, the wind howling around them, dozens of bleached whale and fishbones and skeletons of humans who have made it this far only to die. The **Man** *looks at the* **Boy** *and sees the intense disappointment.*

Man I'm sorry it's not blue.

EXT. DUNES / BEACH – DAY

They sit on the beach wrapped in blankets staring out at a surreal wall of impenetrable smog not far beyond where the waves are breaking. The **Man** *eyes the silent* **Boy***, buffeted by wind, wrapped in a blanket, staring at the empty ocean . . . There is nothing and nobody there. They keep staring out to sea, filled with disappointment. The* **Boy** *impassively surveys the wall of smog which is like an iron curtain.*

Boy What's on the other side?

Man Nothing.

Boy There must be something.

Man Maybe there's a father and his little boy and they're sitting on the beach too.

Boy And they could be carrying the fire too?

Man They could be, yes.

The **Man** *sees the* **Boy**'s *hopefulness reappearing and strokes his head, his heart breaking for him.*

EXT. WATER'S EDGE – DAY

The **Man** *and the* **Boy** *stand with their shoes off. The black sea washes up the sand at their filthy, blistered feet.*

Boy   What are our long-term goals?

Man   'What are our long-term goals?' Where did you hear that?

Boy   I don't know. You said it.

Man   When?

Boy   A long time ago.

Man   When your mother was here?

Boy   I guess.

Man   And what was the answer?

Boy   I don't know.

Man   Well, I don't either.

They stare at the water – charred, quotidian household objects rolling back and forth in the surf.

Boy   Can I go swimming?

Man   Swimming? You'll freeze your nuts off.

Boy   I know.

Man   I don't want to have to come in after you.

The **Boy** *lets the blanket fall and strips out of his parka and clothes. He runs along the beach naked, skinny and white, leaping screaming into the icy surf.*

The **Man** *watches until the* **Boy** *comes out of the water, gasping with cold, shuddering. He wraps the* **Boy** *in the blanket and dries him off.*

EXT. BEACH — EVENING

The **Boy** *is wrapped in blankets by the fire as lightning flickers in the distance, illuminating the empty beach. The* **Man** *drapes another blanket over them. He puts his arms around the* **Boy***, who is shivering and sweating, looking a little wild-eyed, babbling a little.*

Boy   How many people do you think are still alive?

Man   In the world? I don't know. Not very many.

Boy   There could be people alive someplace else. Besides on earth?

Man   I don't think so. They couldn't live any place else.

Boy   Not even if they could get there? If they had a – a – a spaceship?

Man   No. It's unlikely.

*The **Boy** stares, shivering, thinking.*

Man   Are you all right? What is it?

*He cups his hand to the babbling **Boy**'s forehead.*

Boy   I don't feel so good.

*The **Boy** bends away and vomits and the **Man** helps, rubbing his back and wiping the **Boy**'s mouth when he's done.*

Boy   I'm sorry.

Man   That's okay, you didn't do anything wrong.

*The **Man** is very worried now.*

EXT. SAND DUNES – LATER

*The **Man** covers the **Boy** in more blankets and constructs a makeshift tent with the tarp as the rain falls all around.*

Man   It's okay. You're going to be okay. It'll pass.

Boy   Don't leave me here, don't go away, Papa. Not even for a minute.

Man   I won't go away. I'm right here.

*He sits holding the **Boy** tightly. He feels for the **Boy**'s heart. He drops droplets of sugar water from a bowl into the **Boy**'s mouth. As the **Boy** shuts his eyes and dozes he checks the pulse at his neck and wipes his mouth with the blanket.*

EXT. SAND DUNES – NIGHT

*The **Boy** is sleeping fitfully across the **Man**'s lap. The **Man** is still awake, staring in horror as the **Boy** sweats and shakes in his sleep. He wipes the **Boy**'s brow, looks up to the heavens.*

Man   Oh no. No no. Not this. Jesus Christ, what have you done to us? What have you done?

EXT. SAND DUNES – MORNING

*The **Boy** is fast asleep, motionless but for stertorous breathing through his mouth. The **Man** lies beside him, just staring at him, watching him sleep. The **Boy** opens his eyes and focuses weakly.*

Boy   Hi, Papa.

Man   I'm right here.

Boy   I know.

*The **Boy** shuts his eyes and goes back to sleep. The **Man** strokes the **Boy**'s hair tenderly, takes the pistol from his belt and carefully hides it under the blanket by the **Boy**'s side. He stands, takes one last look and walks away . . .*

EXT. SPIT/WATER – DAY

*The **Man** is alone now, staring at the hull of the wrecked boat keeled over in ten feet of grey water a few yards out from the spit – a sixty footer, twin masts. Closer to shore, in the shallows between the boat and the sand, is a grey, lifeless form. The man steps closer and sees:*

Man's *point of view – bobbing about in the tide, the bloated, rotting cadaver of a giant squid, eyes like dinner plates, translucent grey skin like an old light bulb.*

*The **Man** eyes it uneasily, then starts stripping off his clothes. He stares anxiously into the darkly roiling water near the boat. He looks back along the beach to the distant figure of the **Boy**, sitting up wrapped in his blankets, looking*

around, confused and scared, enough to make the **Man**
wince. He collects himself and wades cautiously into the
grey soupy water. He takes a breath and starts swimming to
the boat.

EXT. SAND DUNE – DAY

The **Boy** *is confused as he watches:*

Boy's *point of view – the* **Man** *swimming away.*

Fade to:

EXT. SAND DUNES – DAY

Mystery point of view – over the shoulder of a mystery third
person, camera pushes in slightly on the **Boy** *sleeping.*

EXT. SAND DUNES – DAY

A **Figure**'s *feet enter the scene behind the boy, carefully walk in*
close around the boy. The **Figure**'s *long knife drops into the*
scene, held at the figure's side.

The **Boy** *senses the* **Figure** *and wakes up to see:*

Boy's *point of view – a dark, hunched* **Figure** *standing over*
him. The **Boy** *looks up at the face and, whatever it is, he's*
terrified.

The **Boy** *shrieks, terrified, scrambling away, tripping over pots*
and pans by the fire. He gets to his feet and runs.

EXT. SHORELINE – DAY

The **Man** *struggles from the water and scans the beach, no sign*
of the **Boy**. *He dumps a medical kit and flare pistol he's found*
on the boat and heads for the sand dunes.

EXT. SAND DUNES – DAY

*The **Man** runs over the sand and reaches the spot where he left the **Boy**, the grey tarp blowing away across the beach, the campsite and campfire disturbed. He runs up the dunes.*

EXT. BEACH – DAY

Boy's *point of view – as he looks back he glimpses ragged feet rushing through the sand after him, a pair of hands reaching out . . .*

Man's *point of view – he catches up with the **Boy**, grabs his shoulder with one hand and the gun with the other.*

*Reverse angle – the **Boy** sees it's the **Man** and stops, stares, still frightened, feverish, wild-eyed, confused.*

Man   It's okay –

Boy   A man! There was a man! I saw a man.

Man   It's okay, he's gone now, it's just me.

*The **Boy** collapses, exhausted, into the **Man**'s arms.*

EXT. SAND DUNES – EVENING

*The **Man** and the **Boy** return to examine the disturbed campsite.*

Man   Oh Christ. You stupid ass! You stupid ass!

Boy   What happened?

Man   He stole our shoes. He stole everything.

*The **Boy** goes quiet, forlorn, staring around at the desolation in despair.*

Man   What's wrong?

Boy   I don't know what we're doing.

Man   Come here.

The Road

Boy   I don't know why we're doing this.

Man   Look, there are . . . (*He trails off, lost for words.*)
There are people . . . there are other people and we'll
find them. You'll see.

*The **Boy** just shuts his eyes and slumps on to the sand in
despair. The **Man** eyes him anxiously.*

*The **Man** opens the first-aid kit he took from the boat, takes out
several pills.*

Man   The important thing is that you are getting
better now.

He gently pushes them into the boy's mouth.

Man   Please. Listen to me. Don't lose heart.

*The **Man** seizes the flare gun, takes it from its case
hurriedly, loads it with shells – the **Boy** now watches,
wide-eyed.*

*The **Man** rushes a few paces up the dune and looks over to
where the trolley was hidden – he fires a flare into the air.
The flare arcs up into the murk with a long whoosh and breaks
in a cloud of light, hanging there, hot tendrils of magnesium
drifting down to the sand. The **Boy** watches, curious despite his
despair.*

*The **Man** strains his eyes to see: the dunes bathed in pink light
from the flare and the sand pockmarked with the footprints of
the **Strange Man** in a trail leading to the spot where the
trolley marks trail off into the distance.*

EXT. NEAR BEACH – NIGHT

*Mystery point of view from a distance – a third party is
watching the **Man** and **Boy** bathed in the light of the flare.*

*Camera pushes in on the face watching them – bearded and
scarred, with a wandering eye and a crushed cheekbone, a
veteran of many skirmishes.*

The Road

EXT. SAND DUNES – NIGHT

The **Man** *and the* **Boy** *stand in their bare feet.*

Man   Come on. We have to get our shoes back.

Boy (*frightened, reluctant*)   We don't need them!

Man   We won't get far without them.

They set off hurriedly, in their bare feet.

EXT. COAST ROAD, BLACKENED LANDSCAPE – NIGHT

On the road in the middle of a desolate landscape, the strange lattice of lightning flickering across the dim morning sky, the **Man** *and the* **Boy** *are barefoot on the tarmac.*

Man*'s point of view – way up ahead is the hunched figure seen earlier – the* **Thief***, his back to us, trundling the loaded trolley along the road.*

Man   Come on.

They take off after the **Thief***, bare feet thudding on the tarmac, the* **Man** *in front, the* **Boy** *trailing, trying to catch up. The* **Thief** *looks back at them and speeds up, head bent down over the handle running for his life. When he looks back again the* **Man** *has drawn his pistol and is aiming it directly at him.*

The **Thief** *stops the trolley, pulls a carving knife from his belt, and turns to face them, standing behind the trolley. His face is emaciated and twitchy, a mouth like a bombed graveyard – not the face of the man watching them in the sand dunes. The* **Man** *trains his gun on him, stock still, holding the* **Boy***'s hand.*

Man   Get away from the cart and put the knife down.

The **Man** *spits and brandishes the knife desperately, he's scrawny, sullen, bearded and filthy.*

If you don't put down the carving knife and get away from the goddamn cart I'm going to blow your brains out.

The Road

Boy   Papa?

Man   Be quiet.

The **Man** *cocks the pistol and there's two loud clicks.*

Man   God damn you.

Boy   Papa, please don't kill the man.

Thief   Come on, man, I done what you said, listen to the boy.

The **Boy** *starts crying – the* **Thief** *looks at the* **Boy** *and then the angry* **Man***; this seems to be sobering. He puts the knife in the trolley and steps away, hands in the air, his thumbs are missing.*

Man   How long have you been following us?

Thief   I wasn't following you. I saw the cart on the sand an' I just took it.

Boy   Please, Papa.

Man   Take your clothes off. Take them off, every goddamn stitch.

Thief   Come on, man, don't do this.

Man   I'll kill you where you stand.

Thief   Don't do this, man.

Man   I won't tell you again.

Thief   All right, all right, just take it easy.

The **Thief** *looks at the* **Boy***, who is now covering his ears and the* **Man** *takes an intimidating step closer with the gun.*

The **Thief** *starts stripping and piling his rags in the road.*

Man   The shoes.

Thief   Come on, man.

Man   The shoes.

The **Thief** *sits naked in the road and unlaces the rotting shoes.*

Put them in the cart.

The **Thief** *stands and drops the shoes in the trolley.*

Put the clothes in.

The **Man** *drops the clothes in and stands there covering himself, shivering.*

Thief   Don't do this to me, man.

Man   You didn't mind doing it to us.

Thief   I'm begging you.

Boy   Papa.

Thief   Come on, listen to the kid.

Man   You tried to kill us.

Thief   I'm starving, man. You'd have done the same.

Man   You took everything.

Thief   I'll die out here.

Man   I'm going to leave you the way you left us.

The **Man** *grabs the trolley by the handle, pulls it around, puts the pistol on top and holds his hand out for the* **Boy**.

Man   Let's go.

The **Boy** *doesn't take his hand but they set off along the blacktop, the* **Boy** *snivelling and crying, leaving the* **Thief** *shivering and whimpering.*

Boy   Oh Papa.

Man   Stop it.

Boy   I can't stop it.

Man   What do you think would have happened to him if we hadn't caught him? You've got to learn.

Boy   I don't want to learn!

The Road

Man   I won't be here for ever. Sooner or later you'll have to look after yourself.

*The **Boy** just looks at him – and keeps crying.*

EXT. ROAD/COAST, BLACKENED LANDSCAPE – NIGHT

*Some distance away the **Boy** looks back at the **Thief**, still crying.*

Man   You have to stop crying.

Boy   I can't.

*The **Boy** looks back one last time as the **Thief** disappears from view – still just standing there, utterly lost.*

*The **Man** stops and puts his shoes on. He walks back up the road to the bend but the **Thief** has gone.*

Man   He's gone. Come on.

Boy   He's not gone. He's not.

*The **Man** looks helplessly at the tearful **Boy** as he fits his shoes on for him, the tears streaking the soot on his face.*

Man   What do you want to do?

Boy   Just help him, Papa. Just help him.

*The **Man** looks back down the road, weighing it up.*

Boy   He was just hungry, Papa. He's going to die.

Man   He's going to die anyway.

Boy   He's so scared.

Man   I'm scared. Do you understand? I'm scared.

*The **Man** tries to look the **Boy** in the eye but he keeps his head bowed, sobbing.*

Man   You're not the one who has to worry about everything.

*The **Boy** mumbles, tearful and snotty.*

Man   What? What did you say?

Boy   Yes I am. I am the one.

The **Man** *stops and faces the innocent* **Boy** *angrily, stares, then, relenting, summons all his strength, turns the trolley around and starts wheeling it back the way they came.*

Man   All right. Help me.

The **Man** *takes the* **Boy**'s *hand and puts it on the trolley handle.*

EXT. ROAD/COAST, BLACKENED LANDSCAPE – NIGHT

As the light fades to darkness, they look for the **Thief** *to give him his clothes back and call out 'Hello!' etc. After a moment they stop.*

Boy   He's afraid to answer.

Man   Is this where we stopped?

Boy   I don't know. I think so.

They keep walking, hands cupped to mouths, hallooing mindlessly. The **Man** *stops to rest and watches the* **Boy** *a moment; he has stopped crying as he calls out for the* **Thief**.

Finally the **Man** *piles the* **Thief**'s *shoes and clothes in the road. He puts a rock on top of them.*

Man   Come on. We have to go.

The **Boy** *eyes the clothes sadly, silent now.*

EXT. ROADSIDE DUNES – BLACKENED LANDSCAPE – NIGHT

They find a spot to stop and sit, exhausted. The **Man** *opens the first-aid kit again, selects various pills, crushes them up, pours a cup of water from a jerry can in the trolley, and hands them to the* **Boy**.

Boy   I don't want it.

The Road

Man I have to keep your temperature down.

*The **Boy** swallows the pills and the water, shivering.*

Boy Can I ask you something?

Man Of course you can.

Boy What would you do if I died?

Man If you died I'd want to die too.

Boy So you could be with me?

Man So I could be with you, yes. But that's not going to happen.

*They look at each other a moment, unsure. The **Boy** lies down and shuts his eyes. The **Man** puts a blanket over him. The **Man** walks away a few paces and coughs endlessly, a nagging cough that won't go.*

EXT. ORCHARD — DAY

*The **Man**'s dream — a dream and a memory of an early summer day. The **Man** and the **Woman** are in an orchard, lying in the sun on a picnic blanket, an array of bread, fruit and wine beside them. The **Man** lies back and the **Woman** cradles his head in her lap, stroking his brow. She brings her face down and gently plants a simple kiss on each of his eyelids, then on each of his lips.*

Man's point of view — the **Woman**'s face, smiling a dazzling, radiant smile, framed by sunlight and the indistinct shapes of leaves and blossom and petals against the sky — to him she is angelic. Then he kisses her on each eye and on the lips too, their ritual caress.*

End of dream sequence.

EXT. ROADSIDE DUNES, BLACKENED LANDSCAPE — DAWN

*The **Man** awakes distressed, he wipes a tear, blinks in confusion.*

Man's point of view — the **Boy** is kneeling beside him, watching him calmly, no longer sweating and shivering, recovered.*

Boy   Papa?

*The **Man** rouses himself, sits up and just stares at the **Boy**, amazed, as if he has arisen from the grave.*

Man   How are you feeling?

Boy   I feel kind of weird.

Man   Are you hungry?

Boy   Just thirsty.

*The **Man** gets up and fetches water from a jerry can in the trolley, pours a cup, hands it to the **Boy** who drinks thirstily. The **Man** reaches out and strokes the **Boy**'s hair as he drinks.*

EXT. RESORT TOWN, OUTSKIRTS – DAY

*The **Man** and the **Boy** head towards a seaside town off in the distance.*

EXT. RESORT TOWN – DAY

*They enter a small beach resort with a faded 'Welcome' sign across the road, the **Boy** holding the **Man**'s hand now.*

EXT. RESORT TOWN/WATER'S EDGE – DAY

*They are down by the water. Small pleasure boats are half sunken in the grey water. Faded coloured bunting and painted signs advertise ice creams, food and a fun fair. The **Boy** helps the man push the trolley through the sand until they can go no further. They stop and drop on to the sand, exhausted.*

Boy   Can I tell you something?

Man   Yes.

Boy   You tell me I shouldn't cry but I've heard you crying. I hear you coughing and crying to yourself in the night when you think I'm asleep.

The Road

Man   What of it?

Boy   So if I shouldn't cry you shouldn't cry either.

They look at each other.

*On the port side of town the **Man** wheels the trolley through the deserted docks, past rotten piers, a row of empty wooden warehouses and a rusty red tanker washed up. He is coughing and the sound echoes off the warehouse walls. The **Boy** is trailing a few paces behind; they're not speaking now.*

*As they pass the last of a row of old seaside shops the **Man** slows down to let the **Boy** catch up. But the **Boy** is now studying the ground intently. He bends down and picks up:*

Boy's *point of view – an old cardboard matchbox, its decals faded. He pushes the matchbox open to reveal a perfectly preserved beetle.*

Boy   What is it?

Man   It's a beetle.

Suddenly the beetle twitches, then activates its wings and flies out of the box with a buzz and upwards into the sky.

*The **Boy** and the **Man** stare up at the flying creature, amazed and:*

*Without warning something whistles over their heads very close and hits the wall beside them with a loud clatter. The **Man** lunges at the **Boy**, landing on top of him to cover him and tries to grab the trolley which tips over, spilling everything out.*

*The **Man** desperately tries to take cover while he looks over his shoulder and sees:*

Man's *point of view – in the upper window of an abandoned motel a man is drawing a bow and arrow aimed right at them.*

In desperation the **Man** *covers the* **Boy** *and tries to scrabble away but there's a dull twang of bowstring and an arrow thuds into his leg.*

Man   Oh you bastard! You bastard!

The **Man** *claws the blankets from the upturned trolley aside and scrabbles around for the pistol, but it has fallen from his belt on to the cobbles and scattered out of reach. He spots the flare gun and seizes it, resting it on the trolley and aiming carefully at the empty window. When the lone* **Archer** *appears again he squeezes off a shot and the flare goes rocketing up towards the window in a fiery arc, ablaze with colour, clean through the window. They can hear the* **Archer** *screaming inside and see the coloured light still flaring from the window.*

Boy   Oh Papa!

Man   Stay just like you are.

He gets up and runs limping across the street, the arrow still embedded in his leg.

INT. WOODEN STAIRS – EVENING

He limps up the stairs of the old motel as quickly as he can, flare gun at the ready, arrow in his leg.

INT. WAREHOUSE FLOOR – EVENING

He bursts into the main room and trains the gun. At the far end a **Woman** *is sitting with the prone form of the* **Archer**. *The floor is burnt in a huge patch left by the flare and is still in flames.*

Archer's Woman   You son of a bitch!

Man   Who else is up here?

Archer's Woman   You fucking asshole!

The Road

*The **Man** looks down; his leg is bleeding heavily now and the arrow is still sticking out.*

Man   Where's the bow?

Archer's Woman   I don't have it.

Man   Why are you following us?

Archer's Woman   We're not following anybody. You were following us!

*The **Man** stares at the **Woman**, looking her up and down; she looks sick and thin and desperate. He looks at the **Archer**, lying there dead, his chest and one arm and his face burnt, still smoking. The **Woman** covers his face with the blanket and the **Man** doesn't know what to say, ashamed. He goes.*

EXT. CAFÉ — DAY

*Point of view — again from a distance, as if a third party is watching, we watch the **Boy** and the **Man** hobble into a café.*

INT. CAFÉ — DAY

*One wall of the café is merely a pile of rubble, opening out to the sea. The opposite wall is a photographic mural of lush green woods. The **Man** tries to remove the arrow but just pulls out the wooden stem. He takes off his bloodied trousers and examines the gaping wound with a flap of flesh and the arrowhead, made from a spoon, buried inside.*

Man   See if you can find the medical kit from the boat. Quickly.

*The **Boy** rummages in the trolley, finds the kit and hands it over. He stares as the **Man** slowly extracts the spoon, wincing in agony. The **Man** dowses the wound in antiseptic from the kit and searches through the kit for a needle. He finds a suture needle in a sterile envelope, rips it open with his teeth and, using the light coming in through the parlour windows he threads some silk thread into the needle. He starts to suture up the wound,* *grimacing in pain as the* **Boy** *watches in silence, until eventually commenting:*

Boy Does it hurt?

Man (*stares*) *Yes!* It *hurts!*

Boy What does it feel like?

The **Man** *eyes the* **Boy***, surprised at his inopportune chat.*

Man At least you're talking to me now.

INT./EXT. CAFÉ – NIGHT

They have a campfire in the café by the jetty and sit overlooking the bay, through the missing wall, silent until:

Man Do you want me to tell you a story?

Boy No.

Man Why not?

Boy Your stories aren't true.

Man They don't have to be true. They're stories.

Boy In the stories we're always helping people. But we don't help people. We just shoot people. And in the stories good things happen but we just get sick.

Man We're still here, aren't we? Doesn't that mean anything?

EXT. BOAT LAUNCH – DAY

The **Man** *pulls the trolley slowly, finding it a great effort. The* **Boy** *helps pull, eyeing the* **Man** *with concern. The* **Man** *stops and rests on the trolley and the* **Boy** *pulls on a few more feet then stops and looks back as the* **Man** *coughs for a long painful moment. He takes the bloodstained surgical mask from his face, his breath foggy in the cold; he wrings out the blood and saliva, puts his head between his knees and coughs until he can cough* *no more, gasping for breath, bloody drool unspooling from his lips into the sand like scarlet twine while the* **Boy** *watches, weeping silently.*

Man   We have to leave the cart. I can't push it any more.

EXT. BOAT LAUNCH — DAY

They are trudging along a concrete boat ramp by the beach road, the beach below, the **Boy** *carrying a small suitcase now, the* **Man** *carrying sacks and bags. They stop and the* **Man** *leans, impossibly breathless, his lungs packing up. They stop at the water's edge, where the road reaches the sea.*

The **Boy** *takes his hand gently.*

Boy   What are we going to do, Papa?

The **Man** *can't answer for breathlessness.*

Well, what are we?

The **Man** *sits heavily on the ground, totters as the* **Boy** *stands watching him, eyes welling with tears.*

Oh no, Papa.

EXT. BEACH/DUNES — DAY

The **Man** *is drifting in and out of consciousness in the sand. The* **Boy** *comes over with a cup of water and holds it to the* **Man***'s lips; he drinks. The* **Boy** *has also lit a fire. He spreads out blankets.*

Man   Don't get comfortable. You need to keep going. You don't know what might be down the road.

Boy   No.

Man   We were always lucky. You'll be lucky again. You'll see. Just go.

Boy No. I can't.

Man It's all right. This has been a long time coming. Just keep going south. Do everything the way we did it.

Boy No. You're going to be okay, Papa. You have to.

Man Keep the gun with you at all times. Don't let anyone take it from you. You need to find the good guys, but you can't take any chances. Do you hear me?

Boy I want to be with you.

Man I want to be with you too, but I can't.

Boy Please.

Man You have to go off on your own now. You have to carry the fire.

Boy I don't know how to.

Man Yes, you do. You know everything about it.

Boy Is it real? The fire? Papa?

Man Yes, it is.

Boy Where is it? I don't know where it is.

Man Yes, you do.

Boy Where?

Man It's inside you. It was always there. I can see it.

The **Boy** *stares at him, not sure what to believe.*

Man You have to let me go.

Boy Just take me with you, please. Please, Papa! What should I do?

Man Just hold my hand.

The **Boy** *grips the* **Man***'s hand, bouncing up and down, agitated.*

Boy You said you wouldn't ever leave me.

The Road

Man   I know. I'm sorry.

The **Boy** *falls on the* **Man**, *hugging him tight, face pressed to his chest, sobbing.*

Man   My boy. You have my whole heart. You always did. You're the best guy. You can talk to me and I'll talk to you. You'll see.

Boy   How will I hear you?

Man   You just will.

Boy   How do you know?

Man   You just have to practise. Just don't give up, okay? You'll be okay. You're going to be lucky. I know you are.

The **Man** *closes his eyes and takes deep, rattling breaths.*

Boy   It's okay, Papa. You don't have to talk any more.

Camera pulls back and the **Boy** *is sitting with the* **Man**, *saying nothing. It's starting to grow dark. The* **Boy** *crouches down on the* **Man***'s chest and goes to sleep there, rising and falling with his father's breathing.*

EXT. BEACH/DUNES (CAMP 18) – NIGHT

Darkness all around. The **Boy** *is lying across the* **Man**, *his hand rising and falling on the* **Man***'s chest slowly, irregularly, as the* **Man***'s breath rattles in his lungs.*

EXT. CAR/BEACH – DAWN

Flashback – or the **Man***'s last ever dream. The* **Man** *and the* **Woman** *snooze in the car – an ordinary young couple nestled together in the early-morning sunlight. The* **Man** *wakes and looks at his sleeping wife, smoothes her hair tenderly, very much in love, as she sleeps.*

His hand on her wakes her, she looks at him surprised and pleased, smiles.

Woman   Hello . . .

She kisses him and they look at the blue ocean and the white sand and green sea grass and she puts an arm around him.

Man (*voice-over*) If I were God I would have made the world just so and no different . . . And so I have you . . . I have you.

End of flashback.

EXT. BEACH/DUNES – MORNING

*The **Boy** is awake but doesn't move, his hand still on the **Man**'s chest, now motionless. He looks at the **Man** who is cold and stiff now, long dead. The **Boy** gets up and holds the **Man**'s cold, stiff hand. Tears course down his face silently.*

Boy   Oh Papa. Papa. Papa . . .

EXT. BEACH/DUNES – NIGHT

*The **Boy** is building a campfire. He lights it and sits there watching the **Man**'s motionless body.*

EXT. BEACH/DUNES – MORNING

*The **Boy** has slept beside the **Man**. He wakes, blinks, bewildered.*

EXT. BEACH/DUNES – DAY

*The **Boy** is zipping up the **Man**'s parka carefully and heaping blankets on top, talking all the while.*

Boy   Can I tell you something? I had a bad dream. I had this penguin that you wound up and it would waddle and flap its flippers. And we were in that house we used to live in and it came around the corner but nobody had wound it up and it was really scary because – because – because . . .

He goes quiet as he finishes tending to the body and puts his own parka on, zips it up.

The winder wasn't turning.

He takes the gun, checks the magazine, shuts it and stands, shoving the pistol in his belt.

EXT. WATER'S EDGE, BOAT LAUNCH – DAY

*The **Boy** is standing at the water's edge looking out at the smog and the emptiness. Out of nowhere a man in a grey and red ski parka with the hood up appears carrying a shotgun over his shoulder and a belt of shells.*

*He goes over to the **Boy**; he is the same bearded and scarred man seen earlier, watching them in the sand dunes. The **Boy** doesn't flinch, but his hand goes to the gun at his side. When the man speaks he has some sort of speech defect, possibly caused by missing teeth.*

Veteran   Where's the man you were with? (*No reply.*) Was he your father?

Boy   Yes. He was my papa.

Veteran   I'm sorry.

Boy   I don't know what to do.

Veteran   Well, I think maybe you should come with me.

*The **Boy**'s finger tightens on the trigger of the gun.*

Boy   Are you one of the good guys?

Veteran   Yeah. I'm one of the good guys. Why don't you put that pistol away?

Boy   I'm not supposed to let anybody take the pistol. No matter what.

Veteran   I don't want your pistol. I just didn't want you pointing it at me.

*The **Boy** lowers the gun to his side and the **Veteran** comes a few steps closer, causing the **Boy** to back up a step.*

Veteran   Where's your stuff?

Boy   I don't have much stuff.

Veteran   What have you got? Blankets?

Boy   My papa's wrapped in them.

Man   Show me.

*The **Boy** doesn't move. The **Man** holds out his hand for the **Boy** to take, the **Boy** sees he has a thumb missing and hesitates, wary. The **Man** squats, leaning on his shotgun.*

Veteran   Look. You got two choices here. You can stay here with your papa or you can go with me. If you stay you need to keep off the road.

Boy   How do I know you're one of the good guys?

Veteran   You don't. You'll have to take a shot.

*The **Boy** weighs it up, eyeing the **Veteran**.*

Boy   Do you have any kids?

Veteran   Yes, we do.

Boy   Do you have a little boy?

Veteran   We have a little boy and a little girl.

Boy   How old is he?

Veteran   He's about your age. Maybe a little older.

Boy   And you didn't eat them?

Veteran   No.

Boy   You don't eat people?

Veteran   No. We don't eat people.

Boy   Are you carrying the fire?

Veteran   Am I what?

Boy Carrying the fire.

Veteran You're kind of weirded out, aren't you, kid?

Boy Well, are you?

Veteran Yeah. I am. I'm carrying the fire.

Boy And I can go with you?

Veteran Yes, you can.

The **Boy** *hesitates.*

EXT. BEACH/DUNES (CAMP 19) – DAY

They go over to where the **Man** *lies dead. The* **Veteran** *squats and lifts a blanket to take a look.*

Veteran Are these all the blankets you have?

Boy Yes.

Veteran Is that your suitcase?

Boy Yes.

The **Veteran** *stands and studies the* **Boy***.*

Veteran Why don't you go up on to the road and wait for me? I'll bring the blankets.

Boy What about my papa?

Veteran What about him?

Boy We can't just leave him here.

Veteran Yes we can.

Boy I don't want people to see him.

Veteran There's nobody to see him.

Boy Can I cover him in leaves?

Veteran The wind will blow them away.

Boy Could we cover him with one of the blankets?

Veteran Okay. I'll do it. Go on now.

EXT. BOAT LAUNCH, ROAD – DAY

*The **Boy** waits, and in a moment the **Veteran** emerges from the dunes carrying the suitcase with the blankets slung over his shoulder. He sorts through them and hands one to the **Boy**.*

Veteran   Here. Wrap this around you. You're cold.

*The **Boy** eyes the blanket uncertainly, holds out the pistol for the **Veteran** to hold.*

Veteran   You hold on to that.

Boy   Okay.

Veteran   Do you know how to shoot it?

Boy   Yes.

Veteran   Okay.

Boy   What about my papa?

Veteran   There's nothing else to be done.

Boy   I think I want to say goodbye to him.

Veteran   Will you be all right?

Boy   Yes.

Veteran   Go ahead. I'll wait here for you.

*The **Boy** turns around and heads down to the beach.*

EXT. BEACH/DUNES – DAY

*The **Boy** trudges through the sand over to the corpse of the **Man**, which is now neatly wrapped up in a blanket from head to toe. The **Boy** kneels beside him and starts to cry silently and whisper.*

Boy   I'll talk to you every day. And I won't forget. No matter what. No matter what, Papa.

*The **Boy** dries his eyes, takes a breath, gets up and walks back to the road . . .*

The Road

*As the **Boy** walks out of the dunes holding the gun, a **Motherly Woman** who is standing with the **Veteran** comes towards him.*

Motherly Woman   Oh. I am so glad to see you.

*The **Boy** just stares at her, bemused.*

*A short distance away stands the rest of the family — another **Boy** his own age and a **Girl**. The **Boy** stares at the **Other Boy** and recognises him; it's the same **Boy** he chased earlier.*

*Then the **Boy** notices a threadbare mongrel of a dog, waiting with them.*

*The **Motherly Woman** goes over and puts her arms around him.*

Motherly Woman   We've been following you. Did you know that? We saw you with your papa and we tried to catch up but you were too quick for us.

Veteran   There was some discussion about whether to even come after you at all.

*As she's chatting, the **Motherly Woman** gently takes the gun from the **Boy** and hands it to the **Veteran**.*

Motherly Woman   We're so lucky. We were so worried about you. And now we don't have to worry about a thing.

*She kisses the **Boy** on the forehead and holds him at arm's length and looks at him.*

Motherly Woman   How does that sound? Is that okay?

*The **Boy** stares but says nothing.*

Closing credits.

The Road: Teaching and learning activities

Developing literary and media analysis

The structured, active-learning approaches outlined in the scheme of work enable pupils to build their learning and construct their understanding. Pupils are required to use drama activities to:

+ Analyse writers' complex techniques and skills
+ Understand texts in a cultural and historical context
+ Understand writers' intentions and choices of language, structures and ideas
+ Analyse the different contributions made by novelists, playwrights, directors, narrators
+ Analyse media/visual and literary techniques

Analytical writing at GCSE

Such work has a direct effect on pupils' ability to write about literary and media techniques and use evidence from the text to back up their ideas. Integrated within the work are, therefore, suggestions for further analytical work and GCSE Controlled Assessment responses AQA GCSE English Language Unit 3, part a, and Edexcel GCSE English Literature Unit 3. It is important that the drama activities are not seen as separate from these – they should complement each other. Discussions and written work should be directly informed by drama work resulting in a more detailed analysis and understanding of the text and of the dramatic/media process.

Structuring the activities

The use of drama conventions in isolation will not produce deep learning opportunities. The 'learning' section of the scheme of work is devised in such a way that pupils build their learning and are provided with the appropriate contexts and techniques to produce high-level responses and develop skills. Sharing such an approach with the pupils allows them to have an understanding of 'the bigger picture', vital if they are to become independent, active learners. The scheme of work is addressed directly to the pupil so that they can understand and analyse the learning process and consider the progress they are making in each of the skills identified. Although individual activities are identified within the scheme, they are often inter-linked and inter-dependent and are best approached within the complete scheme of work. Similarly lesson breaks are not identified, as this will be dependent on the length of lessons and nature of the learning groups involved.

Resources

All the resources required, both props and other media, are identified in the scheme of work. Some preparation time is required to ensure that these are available when required. The DVD of the film, *The Road*, is widely available (Icon Home Entertainment, catalogue number ICON 10190). All clips are identified by the appropriate minutes and seconds but for ease of use, a laptop and multi-media projector will allow the clips to be saved as 'bookmarks', a common feature of all media players. It will also enable extracts of the text to be projected on to a screen for pupils to see. If a multi-media projector is not available, then the use of a DVD, TV and overhead projector are also effective for presenting images and text. The film soundtrack is readily available (Mute, catalogue number 5099960770325) but other appropriate music can be substituted in the places identified. Copies of the images/ stills and the full text of the interview with screenwriter Joe Penhall are available for downloading from the Methuen Drama website (www.methuendrama.com) by accessing the page for the Critical Scripts edition of the screenplay. A copy of the novel and/or extracts, as referenced throughout, will be needed.

Use of space

Although some of the activities benefit from a more open environment that allows for a flexible use of floor space, tables and chairs, a drama studio or large space is not required. If space is limited, a classroom can easily be adjusted to enable all the activities to take place.

Dealing with difficult issues

The film does cover a number of difficult issues, which is why it is recommended that this text be used at Key Stage 4, rather than Key Stage 3. It is important that the teacher is aware and sensitive to the issues and considers how these are to be approached with any particular group of pupils. The scheme of work itself has been developed with this in mind and should, therefore, enable teachers and pupils to explore the film in a secure environment, while being able to analyse complex issues, such as fear, death, love and society, in depth.

1. Introducing a context

To interpret words and symbols and reflect on the context that is being introduced.

Learning	Teaching & Resources
✦ The whole class (divided into twos or threes) sits in a large circle, surrounding an inner circle of words (written or printed individually on to pieces of card) which, if read round the circle, make up a quotation from the script.	The words will need to be placed in the correct order before the lesson begins.
✦ As music is played, the teacher will give you an item of clothing. Once all the pairs/groups have an item of clothing, the music will fade and the teacher will read the words on the cards, **'When I have nothing else, I try to dream the dreams of a child's imaginings.'**	♫ Film soundtrack 👔 Props – clothes ■ It is helpful to project the text to allow the pupils to focus on what is being said.
✦ Fold the item of clothing neatly and place it on the floor in front of you.	
✦ In groups, discuss what the quotation might mean and why it might be important to the text. How can it relate to the item of clothing?	
✦ You will be asked to bring the item out to the centre of the circle, a pair at a time, and as you do so, you will read the quotation. At the end of the quotation, complete the phrase 'A child imagines . . .', saying it out loud as you carefully place the	

item of clothing on an ordered pile in the centre of the circle. When the pile of clothing is complete, the teacher will place an unopened, unlabelled food tin on the top of the pile. Music will play throughout.

📼 Props – unopened, unlabelled tin

The clothes and tin are used again in Activities 11 and 15.

🎵 Film soundtrack

Further activities, reflection, analysis or discussion

✦ Discuss the use of symbolism. What do the clothes represent? How might this link to the quotation? Share comments about the quotation. Why might it be important in the text?

✦ Become familiar with the Controlled Assessment Task titles (e.g. explore the ways family relationships are presented; explore the ways writers create a sense of voice) so that you understand the context you are working in. Explore how using such techniques might help develop understanding of how writers use linguistic, structural and presentational features.

✦ Discuss the use of film soundtracks. How did it affect the way the activity was completed?

✦ How was the activity completed with such integrity? What helped you to do so?

2. Exploring the context

To explore and analyse the contrasting settings of the film and reflect on the use of Voice-over.

Learning	Teaching & Resources
✦ Sit in a large semi-circle facing the projected image. Watch the opening shots from the film of summertime in the garden. The teacher will freeze on the shot of the flowers outside the house. What have you noticed from these	✎ Extract from the film (0:00:37–0:01:04) 

shots? What sort of landscape is it? What atmosphere is established at the very start of the film? How? Why?

◆ In groups of four, you are going to develop a Voice-over for these opening shots to explore the place and the people who are seen there. Each group will be allocated a slightly different shot and be told whether they are 'visitors' to the scene or the collective voice of the character(s) within it. Using your still from the opening to the film as a stimulus, develop a Voice-over (spoken in first person in the present tense) that describes the place and your thoughts about being there.

Ensure that the 'visitor' or 'character' Voice-overs are alternated around the circle.

◆ Move in to a space with your group next to a picture. You will be given some time to rehearse your Voice-over in your groups before the process begins.

Copies of the stills from the film to be placed round the room.

◆ Stand with your group in a large circle, surrounding a microphone. When the music fades, the first group will move into the centre of the circle, near the microphone, and provide the Voice-over until the music begins again. The next group will then move into the centre of the circle. This will continue until all groups have provided Voice-overs for the opening shots.

Use the frame forward command at this stage to control the shots displayed.

♫ Film soundtrack
✑ Props – microphone

♦ When all the groups have provided Voice-overs, watch the extract from the film, that covers the following section of the script (pages 4–6)

from What is it? What is happening?
to All the crops are long gone.

⊘ Extract from the film
(0:01:39–0:04:06)

♦ Analyse how the opening shots engage and influence the audience/reader and explore the way in which they contrast with the scenes that follow.

♦ Discuss why the screenwriter/director chose to use Voice-overs and how they relate to the role of a narrator.

3. Exploring a character and role

To analyse a specific scene and character. To explore the screenwriter's skill by selecting evidence to support analysis.

Learning	Teaching & Resources
♦ Sit in a large semi-circle. Read the following extract from pages 25–7 *from* The thunder of a waterfall. The river disappears into space *to* The Man goes back to filtering the water. ♦ Use the Role on the Wall convention to explore the character of Boy. To do this, you need to identify from the extract what you know and select a word that you feel best describes him. Place the selected word on to one of three elemental images (Water, Fire and Earth). You need to think carefully about	■ It is helpful to project the text as this allows the pupils to focus on what is being said. 

which picture to choose and where you might place the word according to the symbolic nature of the picture and what it represents. Justify your choice using evidence from the text.

+ You will return to this Role on the Wall/Element throughout the work by adding words and discussing your previous choices at different stages in the script. You might also want to record your responses, ideas and comments about the script as a whole, on the image, in the same way that is described above. This will provide a useful prompt and recap tool and provide you with a valuable resource when you are planning your written responses to the text.

Use this technique throughout the work to explore the different characters. A permanent display of the ideas produced here can prove a useful learning prompt.

Further activities, reflection, analysis or discussion

+ Work on the three elements can continue throughout an analysis of the script by exploring how the screenwriter, novelist and director use specific techniques to present symbolic ideas or images.

+ Analyse the language devices and techniques used to present the character (AQA GCSE English Language). Explain how language, structure and form contribute to the presentation of ideas (Edexcel GCSE English Literature).

+ You might also want to use the Role on the Wall convention to explore Man. An analysis of the different styles of language used throughout the script can provide an interesting insight into the screenwriter's skill. How does the Man's use of 'maybe' compared with the Boy's more definite statements influence how we see the characters?

+ A detailed media analysis, frame by frame, of this scene can be used to explore the specific shots used and the director's interpretation of the script.

4. Interpreting the script

To analyse the script and explore the choices the screenwriter made regarding the structure of the screenplay.

Learning	Teaching & Resources
✦ You will be working in a small group of two to five pupils. Each group is given an extract from the screenplay.	Group sizes are determined by the extracts.

Extract 1: (pages 12–13)

from Inside a badly damaged trailer home

to He picks up the map pieces carefully.

Extract 2: (pages 24–5)

from Flashback – now the house is in considerable disrepair

to Time for bed, there's a good boy.

Extract 3: (pages 26–7)

from The Man meticulously filters water

to No. There's nothing in the lake.

Extract 4: (page 30)

from Will you tell him goodbye?

to Please don't. Please.

Extract 5: (pages 44–6)

from What is this place, Papa?

to All right.

Extract 6: (pages 48–9)

from Where are you?!

to I hope so.

By exploring these extracts, the pupils begin to select and analyse the relevant information. They also begin to take a real interest in the material and want to know more. By Action Reading the extracts, they have to consider some of the initial issues that directors and actors need to address.

By working on the different extracts in this way, and sharing them with the class through Rolling Theatre, they are essentially teaching each other different aspects of the script.

Extract 7: (pages 57–8)

from Flashback – the Man and the pregnant Woman alone in the house

to He swings it at the frame.

Extract 8: (pages 66–7)

from The Man starts loading cans and packets into a carton

to He carefully covers the surrounding area with debris.

Extract 9: (pages 77–8)

from You know where we are?

to They could be, yes.

Extract 10: (pages 96–8)

from Don't get comfortable. You need to keep going

to It's okay, Papa. You don't have to talk any more.

Extract 11: (pages 98–9)

from The Man and the Woman snooze in the car

to . . . I have you.

✦ In groups, produce a short Digital Video Clip of the extract. To do this, begin with a Still Image, followed by an Action Reading of the script and then freeze at the end in a final Still Image. You need to investigate the script and search for clues about the characters, story and setting in order to produce an accurate Action Reading of the extract.

It is, therefore, not necessary to read large amounts of the script as a whole class. This more active approach leads to more engagement and deeper levels of understanding and analysis.

Past extracts: 2, 4, 7 & 11

Present extracts: 1, 3, 5, 6, 8, 9 & 10

♫ Film soundtrack
Use music to indicate the start and end of the extracts.

◆ As a class, you produce your Digital Video Clips as Rolling Theatre. The teacher will determine which order the extracts should be shown in. Music is used to guide you. All the groups freeze in their initial Still Image and then the first group unfreezes, adds the action and then freezes again. When they freeze, the next group knows that they can begin. This continues with all the groups producing their Digital Video Clip, until all groups have shown their pieces. When you are not presenting your Digital Video Clip, you can become a 'Spect-actor'. This means that while your body remains frozen in the Still Image, your head can turn to follow the action so that you can see and hear the work of the other groups. You should remain in your place, in order for all the groups to freeze in their final Still Image at the end.

Position the groups round the room according to the order needed. The first time through should follow a chronological order, with all the past extracts taking place in order before those in the present. The second time through, move the groups to reproduce the order the screenwriter placed the scenes in, mixing the past with the present.

Further activities, reflection, analysis or discussion

◆ Discuss how the structure of the film script influences our understanding of the narrative, characters and issues. How did the Rolling Theatre activity help to analyse and understand the importance of structure in the script as a whole? Why is the non-chronological order of the script effective? What specific techniques does the writer use to achieve the mixing of past and present and maintain the reader's understanding?

◆ At this stage you might want to analyse specific scenes in detail to explore the different techniques used by the writer and the ways that the director has interpreted this.

For example, why do voices from some scenes appear to be heard over shots from the next scene?

✦ Preparing for the GCSE Controlled Assessments. AQA GCSE English Language Unit 3, part a, and Edexcel GCSE English Literature Unit 3. Analyse how the language devices and techniques are used to explore:

  ✦ Characters
  ✦ Relationships
  ✦ Power
  ✦ A sense of voice

5. Exploring the context

To analyse the techniques used to portray personal and universal (particular and vast) issues and ideas.

Learning	Teaching & Resources
✦ Sit in a large semi-circle facing the projected image. Watch the short extract from the film (developed from the scene described on pages 57–8). Discuss the ways in which the screenwriter and director manage to produce images and ideas that are personal and universal, particular and general. What are they?	✑ Extract from the film (0:27:55–0:28:49) Detailed media analysis is possible, particularly if the scene is compared with the previous one involving the piano (0:48:03–0:50:00)
✦ In your groups, use the extract and the information gained from producing the Digital Video Clip in Activity 4, to select what you feel is the most important line from the extract. How does it suggest both a personal and universal idea? Present a Still Image, which illustrates this line and defines the personal issue. The image can be a literal or symbolic interpretation of the line.	It is useful if they consider ways that the line might be presented symbolically through a Still Image as this helps to understand the symbolism in the film.

- Write the line on a large sheet of paper and place it in front of your Still Image. Think about how the line might be said, while holding the Still Image. Would one character say it, would it be said in chorus, echoed, whispered?

It might be helpful to provide an example of a personal and a universal idea to model the process.

- Now create a Still Image which defines the universal idea that is portrayed by the same line. Think about how the line might now be said.

- All the groups will hold their first (personal) Still Image. The first group will say the line from the extract and then gradually merge from their first Still Image in to the (universal) Image and say the line again. Once they have finished, the next group will know they can begin, saying the line from the screenplay, merging into the second image and speaking the line. This process will continue until all the groups have merged from one image to the other and spoken the lines.

If the chosen lines are retained, they can be added to the Role on the Elements and/or used when analytical writing is required.

- Discuss, as a class, the ways in which the screenwriter creates the different perspectives, the particular and the general, the personal and the universal.

Discuss how this relates to a specific Controlled Assessment task.

6. Analysing a specific device

To analyse the literary, dramatic and media techniques used to influence the reader and/or viewer.

Learning	Teaching & Resources
✦ When the groups freeze at the end of Activity 5, the teacher will read the following extract from the script (pages 97–8) *from* You said you wouldn't ever leave me. *to* Just don't give up, okay?	■ It is helpful to project the text as this allows the pupils to focus on what is being said.
✦ The pupil who has the role of Woman, or who represents her in the 'present', moves to the centre of the circle and forms another small group. This group discusses, for the whole class to hear, what they would like to be able to say to their child, 'Boy'.	Those working on scenes in the present will need to consider who represents the Mother – the boy with her possessions or an alternative character.
✦ After a short period of discussion, the 'women' move back towards their group and say the line to the 'child' in the way they would want it to be heard.	

Further activities, reflection, analysis or discussion

✦ The Mother's Role

✦ The Mother seems to have a greater role in the film than the novel. Further work could be done analysing specific scenes and exploring this idea. The use of film reviews can be effective here.

✦ How do specific images/objects help suggest the Mother's presence throughout the film, even in scenes where she is not on screen?

- ◆ The role of the observer. How is the sense of 'being watched' developed throughout the film? Analyse the media and literary techniques used and the devices that enable the audience to get a sense of being observed.

- ◆ At this stage, you could complete a Role on the Elements for the Mother (see Activity 3).

- ◆ Preparing for the GCSE Controlled Assessments. AQA GCSE English Language Unit 3, part a, and Edexcel GCSE English Literature Unit 3. Analyse how the language devices and techniques are used to explore:

  - ◆ Characters
  - ◆ Relationships
  - ◆ Power
  - ◆ A sense of voice

7. Exploring tension – Conscience Steps

To analyse the different perspectives of the characters and the tensions created.

Learning	Teaching & Resources
◆ Sit in a large semi-circle. Read the following extract from page 69	■ It is helpful to project the text as this allows the pupils to focus on what is being said.

◆ Sit in a large semi-circle. Read the following extract from page 69

   from They come up behind an Old Man, hunched over
   to We've got food we could give him.

◆ Now stand in two parallel lines, facing each other down the length of the room. A member of the class is given the role of Old Man. Using the space between the two lines, Sculpt him into the position you believe he will be in, when the action takes place. Other members of the class are given the roles of

■ It is helpful to project the text as this allows the pupils to focus on what is being said.

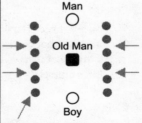

Pupils stand in two lines facing each other

Man and Boy and stand at each end of the room, between the two lines, facing towards Old Man.

✦ As Man and Boy walk down in between the two lines, they will hear their conscience 'speaking' to them. One line of pupils will speak the thoughts of Boy; the other line will speak the Man's thoughts.

✦ You will speak the character's thoughts, thinking carefully about the text you have just explored and what you feel are the character's motivations. Speaking as the father you might say, 'I need all the food for the boy. We're not wasting it.' Or, speaking as the boy, you might say, 'He's starving, we can't let him die.' (Conscience Steps)

The pupils in rows should discuss their ideas as preparation for the task. An example might also be provided.

✦ If Man hears a positive thought, suggesting they give food to Old Man, he will take one step towards Old Man. If, however, he hears a negative thought, he will take a step back away from him. Boy will do the same, depending on the thoughts that he hears.

The characters will need to listen carefully to ensure they are responding to their own conscience or thoughts.

✦ When all the thoughts have been heard, the three characters freeze in the position they are in. The teacher reads the next line of the script, **'He's not getting any food.'**

■ Project the text.

◆ You will be asked who you think would speak next and what they would say. When you (or another pupil) suggest the next line to be spoken, the characters remain frozen, while you go to stand behind the character you will speak for. The line is read again, at the end of which you will speak the next line.

◆ The remaining members of your class are then asked what they think the characters would say next. The individual pupils go and stand by the character that they think they can speak for.

◆ The scene is frozen again, after your teacher has explained that one by one the people behind the Sculpted characters will continue the scene by speaking what the characters say. Using Communal Voice continue the conversation between Man and Old Man, or Boy and Old Man, remembering that at times there may be silences.

◆ As a whole class, read or watch the remainder of this scene (pages 69–70)

from The Old Man looks away, avoiding their eyes
to They walk off the road towards the dead, blackened woods.

It may be more effective to use Communal Voice to explore the conversation between the Man and the Old Man and then Boy and the Old Man, rather than all three characters at once.

It is important that the voices do not speak until they are standing still behind the character they are speaking for.

■ Project the text, or show the ✐ extract from the film (01:01:40–01:03:50)

✦ Was the man revealing his true thoughts when speaking to the Old Man? Was the boy? Did their thoughts or conscience differ from what they actually said? Why? How might the screenwriter have explored the tensions here – Man and Boy, thoughts and speech?

✦ Communal Voice could also be used here to explore a conversation between the author Cormac McCarthy and the screenwriter, Joe Penhall. If the first line introduced by the writer was, 'At this moment I wanted to suggest . . .', then a conversation can be developed to explore the aims and techniques of the different writers.

✦ Analyse what media and literary techniques are used to present perspective, a sense of voice and/or a character's conscience or inner thoughts.

✦ Explain and evaluate how writers use linguistic, grammatical, structural and presentational features to achieve effects and engage and influence the reader/ audience. How do the drama activities help to develop these analytical skills? Refer to specific Controlled Assessment tasks and provide evidence of understanding through analytical writing.

8. The adaptation process

To analyse the adaptation process and the specific techniques and decisions required.

Learning	Teaching & Resources
✦ Sit in a large semi-circle. Read the following extract from the novel pages 173–85 *from* He untied the tarp and folded it back and rummaged through *to* The boy never looked back at all.	▣ It is helpful to project the text as this allows the pupils to focus on what is being said.

◆ You will be working in a small group of pupils. Each group is given a section of the extract used above. Work together to consider how you would adapt this extract in to film. You will need to produce a script and an Action Reading of the film as it is to be acted. Use the knowledge you gained about the screenwriters' techniques, the use of symbolism and how tension is explored.

Extracts from the novel. Depending on the group and time available, you can develop the Action Readings as Rolling Theatre or just develop the script writing process.

9. The greatest fear – presenting an argument with evidence

To analyse how fear is expressed and present a detailed argument, using evidence from the text.

Learning	Teaching & Resources
◆ Working in the same groups and using the extracts from Activity 8, create a Still Image, which shows the boy's greatest fear at this stage in the film. The image can be realistic or symbolic. Choose a line or word which best illustrates this fear and write it on a large sheet of paper and place it in front of your Still Image. Think about how it might be said, while holding the Still Image. Would one person say it, would it be said in chorus, echoed, whispered?	All members of the group need to be involved in the creation of the image. You might provide an example of how a symbolic image can be created in a Still Image.

◆ Now create a Still Image that defines Man's greatest fear. Again, choose a word or line to support this and write it down on a large sheet of paper. Consider how this might be said while holding the second Still Image. What tone and volume might you use? Finally, produce a Still Image and write down a word or line to illustrate Old Man's greatest fear.

◆ All the groups will hold their first Still Image. The first group will say the line from the extract and then gradually merge from their first Still Image in to the Image which presents Man's greatest fear and say the word or line. They will then merge in to their final Image and say the word or line that accompanies it. Once they have finished, the next group will know they can begin, saying the word or line, merging into the second image and third images. This process will continue until all the groups have merged from one image to the others and spoken the three pieces of text.

Depending on the group and time available, you can develop the Action Readings as Rolling Theatre or just develop the script writing process.

♬ Film soundtrack
Use music to structure the piece of drama by playing the soundtrack while the groups merge from image to another.

♦ Freeze again in your image of Boy's greatest fear, but this time taking up positions in a large circle around the room. A large arrow (symbolic of that used in the film) will be placed in the centre of the circle like a clock hand (see diagram below):

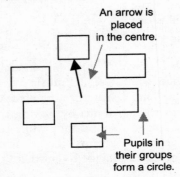

An arrow is placed in the centre.

Pupils in their groups form a circle.

♦ Decide where the arrow would point in terms of which Still Image and text suggests the greatest fear. You cannot speak unless you have first moved the arrow to point in the correct direction. Move the arrow and justify your choice, using evidence from the text.

♦ Other members of your class have to decide whether they agree with this positioning. If they do not, they need to move the arrow to where they feel it is best placed and present an argument, using evidence from the text.

▱ Props – arrow
The use of a flight arrow, as referred to in the screenplay (page 93) allows pupils to explore its significance here.

'Who thinks they have proved that theirs is the greatest fear?' often prompts a response.

It is important that they have to move the arrow first, and have possession of it, before they can speak as this controls the process.

✦ Repeat this activity to explore Man and Old Man's greatest fears.	As evidence is presented to support the comments, pupils are developing analytical skills.
✦ Sit in a large semi-circle facing the projected image. Watch the extract from the film that covers the scenes in Activities 8 and 9 (pages 68–73). Discuss the choices made, and techniques used, during the adaptation process. How has tension and fear been expressed in these scenes?	✐ Extract from the film (1:00:42–1:08:53) Detailed media analysis is possible, particularly if the scenes are compared with their own adaptations.

Further activities, reflection, analysis or discussion

✦ Analyse the media and literary techniques used to present the characters' greatest fears. How are these shared with or felt by the reader and/or audience?

✦ In what ways do the devices used to develop and explore fear also explore the way power is presented?

✦ Explain and evaluate how writers use linguistic, grammatical, structural and presentational features to achieve effects and engage and influence the reader/audience. Refer to specific Controlled Assessment tasks and provide evidence of understanding through analytical writing.

✦ Build up a collection of evidence and significant quotations, linked to the specific techniques and devices the writer uses, to prepare for analytical responses and Controlled Assessments.

10. Placing the Writer and Reader

To explore the techniques used and perspectives developed by the novelist and the ways that the reader can interpret the text.

Learning	Teaching & Resources
✦ Sit in a large semi-circle. Read the following extract from the novel (pages 273–4) *from* They went on. It was already late in the day *to* The thief looked at the child and what he saw was sobering to him.	■ Project the text.
✦ A member of the class is given the role of Man. Sculpt him into the position you believe he will be in, using the space inside the circle, where the action takes place. Think carefully about what facial expression he might have. Other pupils may question this positioning and will re-Sculpt him in to a position of their choosing. Other members of the class are given the roles of Boy and Thief. The characters are Sculpted in to the scene and freeze while the last line is read **'The thief looked at the child and what he saw was sobering to him.'**	■ Project the text and/or provide extracts from the novel.

♦ Another member of the class is given the role of the writer (novelist Cormac McCarthy). Position the writer in the frozen scene where you think he should be. You might use various criteria for this, including the writer's distance from certain characters, the empathy created, the events, the writer's intention and what control the narrator has. Justify your choice, using evidence from the text to support your ideas.

Ask specific questions such as 'Whose eyes is the writer looking through?' or 'Which character is the writer closest to in terms of empathy?'

♦ Discuss the positioning as a class. Throughout this discussion, other pupils should demonstrate the position they feel is most appropriate by moving and Placing the Writer and justifying their choice.

It is important that they physically move the writer, before justifying why.

♦ Another member of the class is given the role of the 'reader'. Position the reader in the frozen scene where you think s/he should be. You might use various criteria for this, including the reader's distance from certain characters, the empathy felt, the events and the reader's understanding of a particular idea. Justify your choice, using evidence from the text to support your ideas. As a class, discuss the positioning of the reader. Throughout this discussion, other pupils should demonstrate the position they feel is most appropriate by moving and Placing the Reader and justifying their choice.

It should be clear that there is no 'right' answer. Pupils are developing their understanding of the writer's techniques and perspective through the arguments and evidence that are presented.

◆ Discuss and model how the analysis and discussion developed through this activity can be directly transferred to analytical writing and the specific Controlled Assessment tasks. This will involve writing about a specific technique and the effect it creates, supported by a quotation from the text as evidence.

11. Editing the script

To analyse the structure of the script and editing process.

Learning	Teaching & Resources
◆ You will be working in a small group of two or three pupils. Each group is given a section or scene from an extract from the screenplay (pages 80–89)	The extract will need to be divided according to numbers in the class. It is important that the sections are not given out in the correct order.
from The Man covers the Boy in more blankets	
to The Boy eyes the clothes sadly, silent now.	
◆ In your group, produce a short Digital Video Clip of the extract. See Activity 4. Each group will be given an item of clothing, used in Activity 1, that they must incorporate into their scene.	✐ Props – clothes
◆ As a class, you produce your Digital Video Clips as Rolling Theatre. You will need to decide as a class which order the extracts are to go in, exploring the editing process used in filmmaking.	

◆ Once the order of the extracts has been decided, each group freezes in their initial Still Image and then the first group unfreezes, adds the action and then freezes again. When they freeze, one member of the group takes the item of clothing and places it in the centre of the circle. They then return to their own group. The next group knows that they can begin. This continues with all the groups producing their Digital Video Clip and placing the clothing in a neat pile until all the groups have shown their pieces.

🖙 Props – unopened, unlabelled tin

Further activities, reflection, analysis or discussion

◆ Discuss the editing process and how this relates to the way in which they decided on the order of the Rolling Theatre. What different techniques or devices were being used? Why? Are these similar, or different to, techniques used by writers in novels?

◆ In relation to the specific Controlled Assessment task, explain and evaluate how writers use structural and presentational features to achieve effects and engage and influence the reader/audience.

12. Placing the Screenwriter. Does the Novelist remain?

To explore the techniques used and perspectives developed by the screenwriter and novelist and the ways that the text can be interpreted.

Learning	Teaching & Resources
✦ The group that has been working on the script extract, adapted from that explored in Activity 10, moves into the centre of the circle. They Action Read the lines and freeze at the end (page 86) *from* Come on, man, don't do this *to* The Thief looks at the Boy, who is now covering his ears and the Man takes an intimidating step closer with the gun. ✦ A member of the class is given the role of the screenwriter (Joe Penhall). Position the screenwriter in the frozen scene where you think he should be. Justify your choice, using evidence from the text to support your ideas. ✦ Discuss the positioning as a class. Throughout the discussion, other pupils should demonstrate the position they feel is most appropriate by moving and Placing the Screenwriter and justifying their choice. Discuss whether this differs from the position of the novelist placed earlier. Why? A pupil representing the 'audience' can	Identify which group has been working on the extract which covers the same details as the extract taken from the novel in Activity 10.

now be placed in the same way and a discussion can take place about the difference between Placing the Reader and Placing the Audience. Is there any? Discuss what this might tell us about the adaptation process.

♦ Read the comments by Joe Penhall, the screenwriter, about this scene. As a class, discuss whether the position of the screenwriter now changes? Why?

When Placing the Audience it is important that it is placed in terms of perspective, empathy and effect rather than a literal positioning in relation to the screen perspective.

■ Project the text.
The full text of the interview from which this passage is taken can be found on the Methuen Drama website: www.methuendrama. com.

Comments from Joe Penhall

I think it's probably a necessary convention of film that the subtext and the overriding thematic concerns be hammered at incessantly. By this point we felt that we needed to show the boy's maturity – the boy is more mature than the father here – and hence the point of the whole journey: the boy becoming a man, if you will. So I made the scene about that, and less about simply getting their shoes back. McCarthy emphasises this too, but in a film you have to hammer it home in order for it to feel climactic, you can't vaguely conceal it and hope smart people pick up on it. The climax of the film can't be 'And then they got their shoes back, but something else is going on here too.' It has to be 'In that moment, the boy becomes a man, the man becomes a boy, the man knows the boy has grown up and yet he is also cowed by it, conflicted, no longer the hero: there is a new hero.' The shoes aren't even the point – the boy shows us what really matters and why we've stuck with them for the entire, miserable, 85 preceding minutes. The exorbitantly priced popcorn we bought and munched through was not in vain after all . . . (Joe Penhall)

✦ The pupil who represented the writer (novelist Cormac McCarthy) earlier should stand at the side of the frozen scene. Should the writer (Cormac McCarthy) be placed into the scripted scene and, if so, where? Does the original writer remain part of the screenplay? Are they left outside the scene? Are they near to the screenwriter or do they have a different perspective? Position the writer where you feel it is most appropriate for him to be.

✦ Discuss as a class whether they agree with your positioning. Throughout the discussion, other pupils should demonstrate the position they feel is most appropriate by moving and Placing the Writer and justifying their choices. Discuss what this might tell us about the adaptation process. Is this the case with all adaptations?

Specific examples can be used here to show where writers have remained involved in the process and where they have completely handed it over.

✦ Watch the extract from the film that covers the scenes in Activity 10.

✒ Extract from the film (1:19:26–1:24:05)

- ◆ Detailed media analysis of this extract from the film enables an exploration of the additional role the director and actors play in interpreting the film script and presenting ideas, tensions and relationships.
- ◆ Compare the different arguments presented to explore writers' ideas and perspectives. Analyse the different linguistic, structural and presentational features used for similar or different purposes. How can this analysis and evidence be included in analytical essays and/or Controlled Assessment task responses?
- ◆ Discuss the significance of the elements water, fire and earth in the film and the use of other symbolism by the writer, screenwriter and director.

13. Placing texts to explore perspective

To explore the techniques used and perspectives developed by the screenwriter and novelist and the ways that the text can be interpreted.

Learning	Teaching & Resources
◆ As a class, read the final scene from the script (page 104).	■ Project the text.
◆ Members of the class are given the roles of Boy, Motherly Woman and Veteran. Sculpt them into the position you believe they will be in, using the space inside the circle, when the final line of the script is said. Two pupils in role as the 'ghosts' of Boy's Mother and Father should be Sculpted on the edge of the scene as if watching.	When placing the 'ghosts' consider where they will be looking and what facial expressions they might both have.

135

+ Place a blank piece of paper in various positions within the scene while asking what text might be found on the piece of paper. Depending on where the piece of paper is positioned, the class should make different suggestions as to what might appear on it.

✎ Props – blank paper Place the paper in a pocket, screwed up on the floor, in a hand etc.

+ In groups, create a piece of text that could appear in any of the places in the scene. It is important that you create two identical versions of this piece of text. You will need to think about how this text might be read or written differently from the perspective of Boy's mother or Boy's father.

+ When you have all completed the pieces of 'text', set up the Sculpted characters again and one by one place one copy of the text where you think it would be found in the scene. You need to remember where you placed your piece of text because you will be reading it out later when one of the characters identifies it.

+ Once all the pieces of text have been placed, Boy's father and mother will gradually come to life and open the pieces of text, one at a time. As they come across each piece of text, they look at the text and freeze. If you placed this particular piece of text you read it out, using the retained copy,

♫ Film soundtrack Play music before, and in between, the reading of each piece of text.

from the perspective of Boy's mother. When you have read it, the mother will pass the text to Boy's father and you will read it again as if from his perspective.	The group might decide to split the group to provide the two perspectives.
✦ The drama continues but stops at each piece of text while different groups read them out, until all the pieces of text have been included.	♫ Film soundtrack

14. Communal Voice-over

To explore the importance of language, contrast and character.

Learning	Teaching & Resources
✦ Return to the Sculpted image, used in Activity 13, but without Boy's mother and father. Sculpt the Other Boy and Girl into the scene. Those pupils not Sculpted, choose a character whose perspective they will explore (Boy, Man, Mother, Motherly Figure, Veteran, Old Man, Thief) and stand round the Sculpted scene in a circle. They will provide the Communal Voice-over. The microphone used in Activity 2 is placed in the centre of the circle.	This activity can be done as a whole class or in smaller groups. ⌨ Props – microphone
✦ Music is used to introduce the Communal Voice-over. When the music fades, a pupil will move into the centre of the circle, near the microphone, and provide the Voice-over that the particular character they represent might provide for this Sculpted scene.	It might be necessary to spend time discussing and rehearsing some of the different perspectives and comments that the Voice-overs can provide before beginning the process.

The next 'character' moves
into the centre of the circle and
creates a voice-over from a
different perspective. Music can
be used throughout.

Further activities, reflection, analysis or discussion

✦ Discuss the use of Voice-over throughout the film and the
different effects it creates. How does this relate to the use
of a narrator in the novel? Is there a narrator?

✦ Discuss how all the drama activities have contributed to
the development of analytical skills. How might these
skills, activities and ideas be transferred to unfamiliar texts
or authors?

✦ Using all the evidence, information and analysis
developed throughout the work, prepare a response to
the Controlled Assessment task or formal analytical essay.

✦ Preparing for the GCSE Controlled Assessments. AQA
GCSE English Language Unit 3, part a, and Edexcel GCSE
English literature Unit 3. Analyse how the language devices
and techniques are used to explore:

✦ Characters

✦ Relationships

✦ Power

✦ A sense of voice

✦ Tension

✦ Openings and Endings

✦ Readers' understanding and emotions

✦ Key themes

15. A child's imaginings

To interpret and analyse words and symbols.

Learning	Teaching & Resources
◆ The whole class (divided into twos or threes) sits in a large circle, surrounding the inner circle of words used in Activity 1, with the items of clothing folded neatly individually in front of them. The teacher reads the words **'When I have nothing else, I try to dream the dreams of a child's imaginings.'**	▱ Props – clothes and unopened, unlabelled tin
◆ You will be asked to repeat Activity 1 by bringing the object out to centre of the circle and completing the phrase 'A child imagines . . . ', as you carefully place the item of clothing on an ordered pile in the centre of the circle. You will need to consider, in response to what you have learnt, whether you want to change how you complete the phrase. When the pile of clothing is complete the teacher will place an unopened, unlabelled tin on the top of the pile and read, **'Just remember that the things you put into your head are forever.'**	When they have finished, the food tin will need to be placed on top of the pile of clothes. ♫ Film soundtrack ■ Project the text.